Royalty
on
Stamps

A celebration of the
British Royal Family through stamps
1952-2011

Est 1856
**STANLEY
GIBBONS**

By Appointment to Her Majesty The Queen
Stanley Gibbons Ltd, London
Philatelists

Published by Stanley Gibbons Ltd
Editorial, Publications Sales Offices and
Distribution Centre:
Parkside, Christchurch Road, Ringwood,
Hants BH24 3SH

© Stanley Gibbons Ltd 2011

Copyright Notice

The contents of this publication is fully
protected by copyright. No part of it may be
reproduced, stored in a retrieval system, or
transmitted in any form or by any means,
electronic, mechanical, photocopying, recording
or otherwise, without prior permission of
Stanley Gibbons Limited. Requests for such
permission should be addressed to the
Catalogue Editor. It is sold on condition that it is
not, by way of trade or otherwise, lent, re-sold,
hired out, circulated, or otherwise disposed
of other than in its complete, original and
unaltered form and without a similar condition
being imposed on the subsequent purchaser.

ISBN-13 978-0-85259-799-6
ISBN-10 0-85259-799-1

Item No. RGSMSP-11

Printed by Advent, Hants.

Dear Reader,

Ever since the Silver Jubilee of King George V, important royal events have been celebrated by stamp issues which have proved to be popular with stamp collectors and, in many cases, with the wider public.

With the news that Prince William and Kate Middleton are to marry, we can, no doubt, look forward to further issues of stamps; indeed, the first Royal Engagement issue, from the Isle of Man, was announced just days after the engagement itself.

We await with interest the announcement of special stamps to celebrate the wedding; and have no doubt that they will provide a fitting memento of the day.

The first stamps to show Prince William appeared shortly after his birth and it is possible, already, to create an attractive collection showing his life to date, a collection which will, of course, grow in the years to come.

Gibbons Stamp Monthly has been around since the reign of Queen Victoria, so it has covered many royal events over the years and has carried a number of articles on the stamps which have been issued to celebrate or commemorate them.

The creation of the *Gibbons Stamp Monthly* Archive this year has allowed us to search our back issues to put together a selection from some of the best of those articles, which we reproduce here, together with a brand new article by former *GSM* editor, John Holman, on the stamps showing Prince William himself – the perfect guide to anyone planning a collection showing his life story so far.

Looking back over the articles in this compilation it is interesting to view past issues through contemporary eyes and to recall some of the excitement that surrounded the events which they celebrated; excitement which no doubt will be repeated in the run up to the 2011 royal wedding.

Whether or not you intend to collect the stamps or covers produced in celebration of the great event, we hope you will enjoy this look back at some of the 'Royal' articles published in *GSM* during the present reign – starting with the Coronation of Her Majesty The Queen – and please look out for our coverage of the 2011 wedding stamps in *Gibbons Stamp Monthly*.

Finally we would like to take this opportunity to wish the Prince and his bride-to-be every happiness in their future life together.

Hugh Jefferies, *GSM* **Editor**

Contents

Prince William: his life on stamps (and a few postmarks)

by John Holman

Shortly after I had finished writing about King Edward VIII (*GSM* January 2011) it was announced that Prince William and Miss Kate Middleton had become engaged and *GSM* Editor Hugh Jefferies asked me to write this article on stamps related to Prince William. Edward VIII was Prince William's great, great-uncle and died 10 years before he was born. Both have been subject to great public interest and media attention. However in philatelic terms, Edward VIII has appeared on relatively few stamps both in his lifetime and since. Prince William, in contrast, has already been depicted on over 100 with more to come.

For those considering a Prince William Collection, this article provides a starting point in terms of what is available. Many of the stamps were part of 'omnibus' Royal issues and in many instances details of the images on the stamps, particularly events, places and dates, are found in the SG catalogue. For other portraits and images such details are not recorded, but with patience the dedicated collector might be able to trace the source through books, newspapers or the internet, or at least make an informed guess as to the likely year the photograph was taken.

Genesis

Prince William's story really begins with the marriage of his parents, the Prince of Wales and Lady Diana Spencer, at St Paul's Cathedral on 29 July 1981. The wedding attracted a vast worldwide television audience, and postal administrations were not slow to issue stamps and related products. Indeed such was the philatelic outpouring that Stanley Gibbons published a catalogue just of Royal wedding issues. Working at Stanley Gibbons at the time, I wrote a booklet *The Royal Wedding and Stamps* and subsequently was involved in the editing of the *Royal Wedding Stamps* catalogue. The British stamps featured a head and shoulders portrait of the couple taken by Lord Snowdon. Although

Lady Diana was as tall as her husband, she was, for reasons of protocol, shown to be shorter on the stamps. There were several omnibus series, featuring portraits and the couple with Royal Yacht *Britannia* from the Crown Agents and other stamp-producing agencies for numerous territories, and other countries produced designs of their own. A Prince William Collection might open with a selection of these numerous colourful issues.

Illustrated above is the miniature sheet issued by the Isle of Man to celebrate the engagement of Prince William to Miss Catherine Middleton

Birth

Just under a year after their marriage, their first child was born at St Mary's Hospital, Paddington, west London on 21 June 1982, and christened William Arthur Philip Louis in the Music Room at Buckingham Palace on 4 August, the 82nd birthday of his great grandmother, the late Queen Elizabeth, The Queen Mother. Four sponsored special handstamps were used on 21 June to mark

61

Birth and christening postmarks from Great Britain and the Isle of Man

his birth, three in London and one at Exeter (these are number 5248–51 in the British Postmark Society's *Special Event Postmarks of the United Kingdom* listing) Three further handstamps, two in London and one in Windsor, commemorated his christening (5344–6). A special Royal Birth slogan postmark was also used by the Isle of Man Post Office.

His birth was marked by an omnibus series from a number of Commonwealth countries, comprising stamps for his mother's 21st birthday (issued earlier in the year) overprinted 'ROYAL BABY' or a longer inscription with name and date. Amongst countries issuing these stamps were Antigua, Belize, Dominica, Grenada, Jamaica, Kiribati, Maldive Islands, Nevis, St Kitts, St Vincent and Tuvalu. In all some 124 stamps and 22 miniature sheets were issued.

The first stamp depiction of the young prince was on issues from Mauritius (SG 647) and North Korea (N2228/MS2242) in September 1982. The Mauritius stamp featured him with his parents leaving St Mary's Hospital, a few days after his birth. Another early image was used on the Isle

A selection of stamps illustrating the Prince's early years

Stamps marking Prince William's birth

Princess Diana with William depicted on an Isle of Man miniature sheet shortly after his birth

of Man miniature sheet, issued in October (MS227). A study of him as a baby was used on a British Virgin Islands stamp, in a series marking his 18th birthday; the stamp depicts him lying on a rug, looking intently at the camera, with wide blue eyes (1042). The photograph was taken at Kensington Palace in February 1983. He is shown as a baby, with a toy mouse on miniature sheets of 2000 from Ascension (MS805) and Cayman Islands (MS392).

That same year, although only a year old, he travelled with his parents to Australia and

New Zealand; the visit attracted considerable media interest and his parents took part in a radio phone-in with children asking questions about their young son. It was revealed that his parents' nickname for him was 'Wills' or 'Wombat'.

Childhood

New Zealand featured him, age two, with his brother and parents on Health stamps of 1985 (1372/4). He is shown at Prince Harry's christening (December 1984) with The Queen, Queen Mother, Duke of Edinburgh, Princess Diana and baby Harry, and the Duke of York on a Samoan stamp for the Queen Mother's 85th birthday in 1985 (701). Other stamps featuring him as a young child were in the omnibus series for his 18th birthday in 2000; these depicted him in Parachute Regiment cap and uniform (Cayman Islands, 931, Solomon Islands MS319), in romper suit (Ascension, 801), wearing a fireman's helmet in 1988 (Falkland Islands, 876 and Fiji, 1097), and in a striped blue tee-shirt and blue trousers (British Virgin Islands, 1043). He is shown playing with his father and brother and with a Shetland pony on Tristan da Cunha's 18th birthday stamps and miniature sheet (883, MS887) and with his brother and grandparents (The Queen and Duke of Edinburgh) on one of Guernsey's Diamond Wedding stamps of 2007 (1178). A 30p stamp from Gibraltar for his 21st birthday shows him, wearing a tightly buttoned overcoat and with a rather pensive expression on his face, alongside his mother (1136). Others show him with Prince Charles, as for example on three values from Kiribati for his 18th birthday (615-7). On the first of these, Prince Charles has baby William, holding a

The Prince with his father, Prince Charles, and on with the Royal Family on the balcony at Buckingham Palace

The Crown Agents birthday issues included miniature sheets comprising five stamps set against a background image of the Prince throwing stones into the river when on holiday in Scotland in 1997. Another image from this time, with his father, was used on a Kiribati stamp (618). The images of father and son were widely used in the press at the time. The stamps and miniature sheets are an important philatelic record of the Prince's younger years and adolescence.

The Prince's first appearance on a British stamp was on one of the four 27p stamps in the miniature sheet issued to mark The Queen Mother's 100th birthday in 2000 (MS2161). The stamps were part of a

koala bear, on his lap; on the 60c. stamp he is pointing something out to the young prince during a trip to Italy in 1985, and on the 75c. they are photographed at Sandringham at Christmas 1992. On a 5s. stamp from Tanzania in 1987 (517), the young prince is shown at the forefront of the Royal Family, gathered on the balcony at Buckingham Palace after the Trooping the Colour ceremony. Another endearing image of the young prince is to be found a stamps from Uganda showing him wearing what appears to be a police cap and uniform (MS2464).

Education
Prince William attended various independent schools and he is shown in a school cap on a stamp in a 21st birthday miniature sheet from Tuvulu (MS1100). In 1995, age 13. he started at Eton College where his mother's father and brother (8th and 9th Earl Spencer) had been educated. Wearing the famous Eton uniform, Prince William is shown on a number of

stamps issued to commemorate his 18th and 21st birthdays—Bermuda (844), Cayman Islands (1018), Falkland Islands (952), and Gibraltar (1137). At Eton he became captain of his house football team. He is noted as a keen sportsman, also enjoying polo, water-polo, swimming, basketball, and other activities.

18th birthday
Although there were no British stamps on this occasion, there were plenty of issues elsewhere. The Isle of Man produced a miniature sheet of five stamps showing images of William as a child, with The Queen Mother and with his father and brother (MS894), and Jersey issued four 75p values showing him in ski outfit in the Alps, playing polo, and against images of Beaumaris Castle, Anglesey (near where he is now stationed in the RAF), and of celebratory fireworks (955/8).

Prince William at Eton

Celebrating the Prince's 18th birthday

photograph of four generations: The Queen Mother, The Queen, Prince Charles, and Prince William, taken by John Swannell on the occasion of The Queen Mother's 99th birthday. The photograph shows just how tall the Prince is, standing alongside his grandmother.

After Eton the Prince enjoyed a gap-year travelling and working in Belize, Chile and Africa, before going up to St Andrew's, Scotland's oldest university, in 2001 to study Art History. Later he changed to study Geography. At St Andrew's he was known to other students as 'Steve' to try to preserve his privacy, and it was whilst a student that he met Kate Middleton, now to be his wife.

The Prince depicted on British stamps

21st birthday

Whilst at university he celebrated his 21st birthday, which gave rise to a number of commemorative stamps. Royal Mail issued four stamps showing close-up photographs of Prince William on his first day at university in September 2001 (28p), at Highgrove, his father's house, in September 2000 (E stamp, European rate), on a visit to Anchor Mills, Paisley, Scotland, in September 2001 (47p), and on a visit to Glasgow, also September 2001 (68p). On three of the four stamps he is looking straight to camera, on the 47p he glances to his left, possibly looking towards the press or a crowd of well-wishers. On the first two studies he is casually dressed in a pullover, on the

Some 21st birthday issues

other two, being on official visits, he wears a jacket, shirt and tie. The stamps reproduce the portraits in black and white against rather dull coloured backgrounds giving overall a somewhat sombre look. In none of the images does the Prince look especially happy; on the 28p stamp he is looking up at the camera and appears to have a slightly sinister expression. In my view, the E stamp was the best of the four and it was a pity none were captioned to indicate the reason for issue. The much more joyful Crown Agents issues were clearly and helpfully fully captioned with the event and date.

I was working for Royal Mail at the time of the issue and recall some correspondence about the cropping of the photographs for the stamps, cutting off the top of the Prince's head. One person phoned me and in strong terms complained we were insulting the future king. I politely pointed out that the stamps had been approved by the Prince and his grandmother and the caller responded with 'well if they have approved them, who am I to disagree' before ringing off.

As well as the official 'First Day of Issue' postmarks for Tallents House and Cardiff, no fewer than 17 sponsored special handstamps were used on first day covers for this issue. These were for places associated with the Prince—London W2 (showing the hospital where he was born), St Andrews (university), and Windsor. There was even a special postmark for Fort William in Scotland. The presentation pack for the issue featured photographs of the Prince in each year from 1982 to 2002, and also reproduced his coat of arms, granted for his 18th birthday in 2000.

The birthday stamps from Crown Agents territories featured black and white photographs of the Prince, formal or informal, together with smaller colour photographs of him playing sports or relaxing. These images include him playing polo on British Virgin Islands, British Indian Ocean Territory, Falkland Islands (with Prince Harry), and Tristan issues, and in ski outfit, putting his arm around his father's shoulder on the £1 value of BIOT. On one of the Ascension stamps, he is shown raising his hand to his ear, possibly feigning hearing a question from the press. The black and white portraits show him in a variety of poses—serious (Ascension and Falkland

7

Prince William with his great grandmother, Queen Elizabeth The Queen Mother

Portraits

Virtually all of the images of Prince William used on stamps have been photographs. One exception is an image of him on a stamp from Niue, pictured with The Queen Mother to respectively commemorate their 18th and 100th birthdays. The stamp (880) bears what appears to be hand-drawn images although probably based on photographs. The name of the designer is not given in the SG catalogue.

A hand-drawn portrait of the Prince and John Wonnacott's portrait showing William with members of the Royal Family

Islands), thoughtful (South Georgia), and playful (British Virgin and Falklands Islands). They all capture the mood of a young man at an important juncture in his life. The double-image 21st birthday stamps are a particularly good record of the Prince at work and play and include images at Tidworth and Cirencester Polo Clubs, at the Queen Mother's 101st birthday at Holyroodhouse, Edinburgh, at Sighthill Community Education Centre, and on the Raleigh International Expedition.

Guernsey produced a strip of ten stamps with images of William from baby to playing polo in 2002, including studies at Eton and on a community project in Chile (998/1007). Jersey issued a miniature sheet containing a superb £2 stamp showing the Prince with his father and The Queen (MS1106), and the Isle of Man four stamps (1074/7) reproducing photographs in black and white but with the Prince looking rather happier than on Royal Mail's quartet. The front cover of the presentation pack for this Isle of Man issue, entitled 'The People's Prince', bears an attractive photograph of William with Arthur's Seat in Edinburgh as the background.

Since leaving university the Prince has begun to carve out a role for himself during the wait (and it might be a long one) before he becomes King. In 2003 he was appointed a Counsellor of State, able to undertake duties for The Queen whilst she is overseas. In 2005 he went to represent his grandmother at World War II commemorative ceremonies in New Zealand, returning then in 2010 to open the Supreme Court of New Zealand building. Like his father and brother, he has served in the military, having trained in all three services at Sandhurst, RAF Cranwell, and Britannia Naval College Dartmouth. He is currently serving in the RAF, on Sea King helicopters in the Search and Rescue operation based at RAF Valley on Anglesey.

The Prince, like his late mother, is keen to support charities and follows her as Patron of Centrepoint, a charity for the homeless, and of the Royal Marsden Hospital. He is also Patron of the Tusk Trust involved in wildlife conservation and community development in Africa. His interest in sport is represented by his being President of the (English) Football Association, and Vice Royal Patron of the Welsh Rugby Union. With Prince Harry he attended England matches in the World Cup in South Africa last year, but sadly the Royal presence did not improve the team's performance.

One of my interests other than philately is Royal portraiture, so I particularly like the Isle of Man issue for The Queen's Golden Jubilee in 2002 which reproduces four painted portraits of The Queen and one of the Royal Family. This last (974) is by John Wonnacott and was done to mark The Queen Mother's 100th birthday in 2000. It is a well-known portrait and features The Queen Mother (seated) surrounded by The Queen, Duke of Edinburgh, Prince Charles, and William and Harry, plus a number of Royal corgis. Prince William is prominent in the foreground, and, somewhat controversially, had his hands in his pockets. The 12-foot high portrait was done in the White Drawing Room at Buckingham Palace and is highly reminiscent of a much more formal painting of George V and his family in the same room, painted by Sir John Lavery in 1913. I hope that one day the fine new painting of Princes William and Harry, in dress uniform of the Household Cavalry Blues and Royals, unveiled in January 2010, will appear on stamp. The portrait was painted by Miss Nicky Philipps for the National Portrait Gallery, London.

Most of the images described here are on stamps commemorating the Prince himself. However he also features on other Royal issues, principally those for The Queen Mother's 100th birthday in 2000. The Crown Agents produced a tasteful series of stamps entitled 'The Queen Mother's Century' showing her and national/international events during her long life. Some of the stamps portrayed her with members of the Royal Family and William appears on stamps from Cayman Islands (also with his father), Falkland Islands (also father and brother), Norfolk Island (also The Queen), South Georgia, Tristan da Cunha (in family group), and Tuvalu (also Prince Harry). A handsome series of miniature sheets was also issued by the Crown Agents as a tribute to The Queen Mother following her death in 2002. Each sheet contained two stamps plus images in the borders. The sheet from South Georgia included a nice image of her with Prince William leaving church—I think at Sandringham. In this photograph, the affection of great-grandmother and great-grandson is plain to all.

One of the most interesting Royal sets of recent years was issued by Gibraltar in 2009, featuring all eight of the grandchildren of The Queen and Duke of Edinburgh, including Prince William (1324/31).

I think all of the stamps showing the Prince have been printed in gravure or lithography, the predominant modern methods of production. However, in my view, the best portrait stamps are those produced in recess (intaglio) printing, as for example many fine stamps from Monaco and Sweden. Although recess printing is expensive, and there are

few skilled stamp engravers to call on to do the work, may one hope that at some time we will have a engraved image of Prince William on a stamp. If well executed, it would be the centrepiece of any Prince William stamp collection.

Marriage

Now the Prince enters a new stage in his life. On 19 October 2010 he proposed to Kate Middleton, his girlfriend since university days, at the Lewa game reserve in Kenya. After obtaining The Queen's permission to marry (required by law), the engagement was announced from Clarence House on 16 November to wide acclaim from politicians and the media. Next day one national broadsheet newspaper devoted no less than 16 pages to the story of the engagement. A week later it was announced that the wedding will take place at Westminster Abbey on 29 April 2011.

The Isle of Man Post Office were quick off the mark, with an Engagement issue on 26 November. This comprised a miniature sheet containing two monochrome £1.50 stamps showing Prince William against two background colour photographs of him and Miss Middleton and a further image of Miss Middleton. Royal Mail announced it would issue stamps showing the couple and no doubt there will be issues from Commonwealth countries. However I do not expect issues on the scale of those in 1981 for the wedding of Charles and Diana and doubt that few collectors would welcome such.

Prince William gave his fiancée his mother's sapphire engagement ring which can be seen on the engagement picture of

Prince Charles and Lady Diana used on the top values in the Crown Agents omnibus series for the Royal Wedding in 1981. The 18-carat white gold ring contains an oval sapphire surrounded by a cluster of 14 diamonds, supplied by Garrard, the crown jewellers. Miss Middleton described the ring as 'very, very special'.

The Future

It is expected that the Prince and his bride will be granted a Royal title on their marriage, possibly as Duke and Duchess of Clarence, Cambridge, or Sussex—all Royal ducal titles. When his father becomes King, William will inherit his titles as Duke of Cornwall and (in Scotland) Duke of Rothesay. Eventually he will become King, possibly taking the title William V or another name of his choosing. Edward VIII's first name, it should be remembered was David, and George VI's was Albert.

Prince William and Miss Middleton will now be for ever in the spotlight but hopefully will be allowed some privacy after their wedding. The Prince was the subject of a TV 'biopic' film, *Prince William*, in 2002, in which he was played by Jordan Frieda, son of pop-singer Lulu. The film was based on his life between the time of the death of his mother and his going to university. No doubt he will be portrayed in further films and TV programmes in future yeas.

What is sure, however, is that he will feature on more stamps and as this article has shown there is already a significant number to start a Prince William Collection. One day he will inherit the world's most famous (and probably most valuable) stamp collection, the pride and joy of his great, great-grandfather, King George V. The Queen, as Princess Elizabeth in 1946, is shown looking at one of the many albums in the Royal Philatelic Collection on a South Georgia stamp of 2002 (334).

The many duties that William will have to carry out as King are depicted on the most pleasing 'A Royal Year' issue from the Solomon Islands in 2005 (1138/49). These show The Queen taking part in the following activities: Order of the Garter ceremony, Trooping the Colour, Royal Ascot, Garden Party, Royal Visits, State Visits, State Opening of Parliament, Remembrance Day, Investitures, Christmas Broadcast, Maundy Service, and Chelsea Flower Show.

The Isle of Man has also issued stamps depicting Royal duty and service, to mark The Queen's 80th birthday in 2006. One of the eight stamps depicts Her Majesty with Prince William on the balcony of Buckingham Palace—an endearing, smiling study of grandmother and grandson, present and future monarch (1276).

Royal Wedding stamps

I conclude this article with illustrations of some Royal Wedding stamps of the past. In 1947 Great Britain celebrated the wedding of Princess Elizabeth and Prince Philip (The Queen and Duke of Edinburgh) with just a special slogan postmark. Stamps were issued by Australia and Canada, although both depicted only the Princess, not her husband. The following year stamps were issued by Great Britain and Empire (Commonwealth) countries to mark the silver wedding anniversary of King George VI and Queen Elizabeth, and a further silver wedding issue commemorated that of The Queen and Duke

One day the Prince will inherit the Royal Philatelic Collection

Royal duty: Some of the many duties William will have to carry out when he becomes King are depicted on a set of stamps from the Solomon Islands

Present and future monarchy: Prince William with The Queen

of Edinburgh in 1972, followed by more for their 50th, and 60th anniversaries in 1997 and 2007.

William's parents on their engagement with detail showing his mother's ring which the Prince has given to Miss Middleton

There were numerous issues for the weddings of all four of The Queen's children—Princess Anne (to Mark Phillips) in 1973, Prince Charles (to Lady Diana Spencer) in 1981, Prince Andrew (to Sarah Ferguson) in 1986, and Prince Edward (to Sophie Rhys-Jones) in 1999. Sadly three of these marriages have subsequently been dissolved. There were a limited number of issues for Prince Charles's second marriage (to Camilla Parker Bowles) in 2005. It will be interesting to compare the wedding stamps for Prince William and Miss Middleton to the earlier issues. We wish them well.

Readers interested in Royal issues are recommended to the British Royal Portraits Stamp Group, details of which are available from Cyril Parsons, 83 Ingram Avenue, Aylesbury HP21 9DH. The Group publishes a useful Newsletter with listings and features on Royalty stamps, both British and overseas.

Royal weddings and anniversaries of the past

The People's Prince: The Isle of Man presentation pack issued to mark William's 21st birthday shows him with Arthur's Seat in Edinburgh as the background

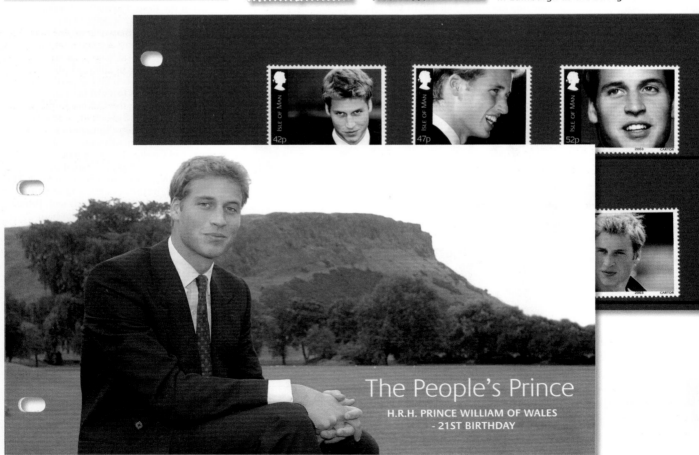

The People's Prince

H.R.H. PRINCE WILLIAM OF WALES - 21ST BIRTHDAY

THE ROYAL ENGAGEMENT
A Special double FDC and Announcement cover

BCE08DBL
£12.95

16 NOV '10

Only 250 produced most sold already but some have been reserved for Stanley Gibbons readers The Isle of Man Post Office issued a special miniature sheet for the Engagement on the 26th November.

Postmarked on 16th November
- the day of the announcement

Postmarked on 26th November
- the first day of issue of the Isle of Man miniature sheet

These will be very scarce. Each cover costs just £12.95

THE ROYAL WEDDING: We will be producing some fantastic FDC's on April 29th. No details yet of the special stamps. Full details will be in our Cover Lover magazines, on our website www.buckinghamcovers.com or via our special email service "Hear it First"

FIRST ACTUAL STAMP

Gibraltar has won the race for issuing the first Buckingham Palace approved new stamp. We have spilt our covers and have limited the IOM double to 250 (almost sold out) and 250 of these. We would expect these to sell out before Christmas so recommend early booking. Limit of 3 per customer.

In addition to the superb sheet we have located 200 Kenya stamps and have cacheted them for the October engagement

16 NOV '10

BCE08DBL2
£12.95

Keep informed of all the latest Buckingham releases at **www.buckinghamcovers.com**

KING EDWARD VIII ACCESSION

Commemorating the accession of Edward VIII this cover will have a Caernarfon Castle stamp (Prince of Wales) postmarked at Windsor on the 20th January 2011 the 75th Anniversary. Our coin is a rare unofficial crown struck many years ago. It also has the complete set of King Edward VIII 1936 stamps with a special cachet. Also available signed by Edward Fox.

BCC123
£16.95

Rare Royalty Items at Incredible Prices

ROY11A
£350

QUEEN MOTHER SIGNED CARDS

We have a wonderful selection of signed Royalty items including this card featuring a photo taken at Mey. More items like this available

WE ARE SPECIALISTS IN ROYALTY AND ALWAYS HAVE AN AMAZING RANGE OF UNUSUAL ITEMS CALL SARAH, BETH, SIOBHAN OR SUE ON 01303 278137 FOR MORE INFORMATION

Please Return to: Buckingham Covers, Warren House, Shearway Rd, Folkestone, Kent. CT19 4BF Tel: 01303 278 137
Fax: 01303 279 429 E-Mail: betty@buckinghamcovers.com

CODE	DESCRIPTION	QTY	PRICE
BCE08DBL	Isle of Man, Mini-sheet FDC & Announcement DBL		£12.95
BCE08DBL2	Gibraltar FDC & Announcement DBL + Kenya stamp		£12.95
BCC123	Edward VIII Accession Coin Cover		£16.95
BCC123S	Edward VIII Coin Cover - Signed by **Edward Fox**		£26.95
ROY11A	**Queen Mother** Signed Christmas Card - Mey		£350
Postage, packing & insurance per sending			£1.95
Special Delivery (recomended for orders over £100)			£4.95
For interest free split payments, call 01303 278137.		Total	

I enclose my Cheque/Postal Orders made out to Buckingham Covers or £ . . . OR please debit £ . . . . from my credit/debit card number:

Expiry Date   Issue No/Start Date

Signature

Security Code*   *Last 3 digits on back of card. We cannot process your order without it.

Title (Mr/Mrs/Miss/Ms)   Initial

Name

Address

Post Code   Daytime Tel No

Personal Email

Source: 51   Media: GSM1012

Evocative Royal Diamond Wedding Stamps Capture Atmosphere of 20 November 1947

HM The Queen and HRH The Duke of Edinburgh celebrate their Diamond Wedding Anniversary on 20 November. It is a great opportunity to start an absorbing new thematic collection as Peter Jennings FRPSL, FRGS, explains in this special report

On Monday 19 November, HM The Queen and HRH The Duke of Edinburgh will attend a special Service of Celebration at Westminster Abbey, on the occasion of their Diamond Wedding Anniversary. The Royal Wedding of Princess Elizabeth to Lieutenant Philip Mountbatten RN took place in Westminster Abbey, London, on Thursday, 20 November 1947.

Princess Elizabeth met the man who was to become her husband on 22 July 1939 during a visit by the Royal Family to the Royal Naval College at Dartmouth. She was 13 years old. He was Philip, Prince of Greece and Denmark, a nephew of Lord Louis Mountbatten, the last Viceroy of India, who acted as an escort to the two princesses, Elizabeth and Margaret. He was 18 and a cadet at the college.

Philip was born on 10 June 1921 on Corfu, but at the age of 18 months, due to political instability, he and his family were evacuated from the island to Paris. He was educated in France, Germany and England and began his naval career in 1939 at the Britannia Royal Naval College in Dartmouth.

During the Second World War in 1940, he served as a midshipman on board HMS *Ramilles* and in 1941 was transferred to HMS *Valiant*, a battleship stationed in Egypt. Later in the war he was promoted to the rank of Lieutenant and saw service during the allied invasion of Sicily and was present on board HMS *Whelp* at the surrender of the Japanese Forces in Tokyo Bay.

Philip continued to visit Windsor during the war years and the romance between the couple blossomed. The engagement was announced by King George VI on 10 July 1947. A notice was attached to the railings of Buckingham Palace: 'It is with the greatest of pleasure that the King and Queen announce the betrothal of their dearly beloved daughter, The Princess Elizabeth, to Lieutenant Philip Mountbatten, R.N., son of the late Prince Andrew of Greece and Princess Alice (Alice of Battenberg), to which the King has gladly given his consent'.

Honeymoon

The day after the wedding ceremony, recorded and broadcast by the BBC, King George VI created Philip, 'Duke of Edinburgh'. Princess Elizabeth and Prince Philip spent their honeymoon at Broadlands, Romsey, Hampshire, the home of Lord Mountbatten,

The engagement was announced by King George VI on 10 July 1947

and at Birkhall, the Royal estate in Royal Deeside, Aberdeenshire.

After the wedding, the Royal couple moved into Clarence House in London and the Duke of Edinburgh returned to his naval career. He rose through naval ranks to Lieutenant Commander and commanded HMS *Magpie*, a frigate.

The death of King George VI on 6 February 1952, and the accession of Princess Elizabeth to the throne, ended Prince Philip's naval career. He now had a new role as consort of the monarch.

His support for The Queen during their 60 years of marriage has been unstinting. They have attended state visits together, received foreign dignitaries and carried out numerous formal and informal duties. HRH Prince Philip established the Duke of Edinburgh's Award in 1956, and this remarkably successful scheme now operates in more than 100 countries throughout the world. He was President of the World Wide Fund for Nature from 1981 to 1996. Now as President Emeritus, he still works actively on behalf of the organisation.

Guernsey
Date of issue: 2 August 2007.
Values: 32p, 37p, 45p, 48p, 50p, 71p.
Photographer: Mark Whyte.
Printer: Joh Enschedé.
Process: Offset lithography with pearlescent ink.

• •

Check list of Royal Diamond Wedding stamps issued during 2007

Royal Mail
Date of issue: 16 October 2007.
Values: 2×1st, 2×54p, 2×78p, *se-tenant* pairs.
Design: Studio David Hillman.
Printer: Cartor Security Printing.
Process: Lithography.
Royal Mail's first self-adhesive miniature sheet—four stamps, 2×1st, 69p, 78p. Price £2.15.
Design: Studio David Hillman.
Printer: Walsall Security Printing.
Process: gravure.

The six stamps depict HM The Queen and HRH Price Philip at a series of formal events and the miniature sheet shows four informal images which appear 'scattered' on a pile of other family photographs. The sheet features an exclusive newly commissioned photograph taken by Lord Snowden of HM The Queen and HRH The Duke of Edinburgh. A Presentation Pack containing both the mint stamps and miniature sheet is available, price £6.

Stamps
The stamps show: 2×1st—The Queen and Prince Philip leaving St Paul's Cathedral after a thanksgiving service for her 80th and his 85th birthdays in 2006 and The Queen and Prince Philip inspecting the King's Troop Royal Horse Artillery in Regents Park on 30 April 1997. 2×54p—The Queen and Prince Philip at the Garter Ceremony, Windsor, on 16 June 1980 and The Queen and Prince Philip at Royal Ascot, 1969. 2×78p—The Queen and Prince Philip at the premier of *The Guns of Navarone*, 27 April 1961 and Princess Elizabeth and Lieutenant Philip Mountbatten RN at Clydebank, 1947.

Miniature sheet
The miniature sheet depicts informal images of the Royal Family: 1st—The Royal Family at Balmoral, 1972. 1st—The Queen and Prince Philip photographed at Buckingham Palace by Lord Snowdon, 2007. This picture was specially commissioned. 69p—The Royal Family at Windsor Castle, 1965. 78p—Princess Elizabeth and Prince Philip with Prince Charles and Princess Anne at Clarence House, 1951.

Jersey

Date of issue: 20 November 2007, the anniversary date.
Value: £3 issued in a souvenir 'Royal Diamond Wedding Anniversary' sheetlet of four stamps depicting HM Queen Elizabeth II and HRH The Duke of Edinburgh.
After 12 months this stamp will become the £3 value in the current range of definitives.
Artist: Andrew Robinson.
Printer: Cartor Security Printing.
Process: Offset lithography.

Isle of Man
The Isle of Man was the first country to issue special stamps to commemorate the Royal Diamond Wedding, entitled 'A Lifetime Partnership'.
Date of issue: 22 February 2007.
Values: strip of 6×60p.
Designer: EDL Design.
Printer: BDT International Security Printing.
Process: Offset lithography.

Crown Agents Stamp Bureau

The layouts were produced by CASB Studio and the stamps were printed in offset lithography by BDT International Security Printing Ltd in Dublin. The issues comprised four values printed in decorative sheetlets of six stamps. The souvenir sheet comprised one single stamp. The images were sourced primarily from the *Illustrated London News* but the CASB also used Camera Press.

The following United Kingdom Overseas Territories are taking part in the issue:

British Indian Ocean Territory
Release date: 1 June 2007.
Values: 2×54p, 2×90p and souvenir sheet £2.14.

St Helena
Release date 26 April 2007.
Values: 25p, 35p, 40p, £2 and souvenir sheet £2.

Tristan da Cunha
Release date: 1 June 2007.
Values: 4×50p and souvenir sheet £2.

Other countries taking part in the Crown Agents omnibus are:

Bahamas
Release date: 1 June 2007.
Values: 15c., 25c., 50c., 65c. and souvenir sheet $5.

Cayman Islands
Release date: 12 September 2007.
Values: 50c., 75c., 80c., $1 and souvenir sheet $2.

Kiribati
Release date: 31 October 2007.
Values: 50c., 75c., $1, $1.50 and souvenir sheet $5.

Nauru

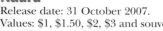

Release date: 31 October 2007.
Values: $1, $1.50, $2, $3 and souvenir sheet $5.

Pobjoy Mint

Pobjoy Mint Ltd now has the agency for the following two UK Overseas Territories:

Ascension

Release date: 2007.
Values: 35p, 90p, £1.25, triptych format.
Artist: Andrew Robinson.
Printer: BDT International Security Printing.
Process: Offset lithography.
35p Princess Elizabeth and Philip Mountbatten photographed for the first time after publicly announcing their engagement in July 1947. 90p a reproduction of the Wedding Programme, a treasured souvenir of a special day. £1.25 Queen Elizabeth II and Prince Philip, Duke of Edinburgh arrive at St Paul's Cathedral for a service of thanksgiving held in honour of the Queen's 80th birthday (photographer Tim Graham).

Falkland Islands

Release: 20 November 2007.
Value: £1.
Artist: Andrew Robinson.
Printer: BDT International Security Printing.
Process: Offset lithography.

Other Commonwealth countries issuing special stamps to commemorate the Royal Diamond Wedding are:

Solomon Islands

Release date: 31 January 2007.
Values: $2.10, $2.50, $5, $20 and souvenir sheet $20.

Gibraltar

Issue Date: 28 February 2007.
Values: 40p, 42p, 66p, 78p and souvenir sheet £1.60.
Designer: Stephen Perera.
Printer: Lowe-Martin Security Printers.
Process: Offset lithography.

New Zealand

Issue Date: 5 September 2007.
Values: 50c., $2.00.
Designer: Communication Arts, Wellington.
Printer: Southern Colour Print.
Process: Litho.

Australia and Canada have not issued stamps to mark this particular anniversary.

The Queen's 80th Birthday Celebrated in Stamps

Peter Jennings FRPSL, FRGS reviews the Crown Agents omnibus stamp issue and talks to royal photographer, Tim Graham, who provided several of the photographs

Her Majesty The Queen celebrates her 80th Birthday on Friday 21 April. To commemorate this important anniversary, the Crown Agents Stamp Bureau is releasing an engaging omnibus of special stamps and philatelic souvenir sheets.

The stamps depict a thoughtful selection of both formal and informal portraits taken during her life, and supplied by a number of agencies—Alpha, Hulton, Press Association, Rex Features—and by Tim Graham, the distinguished royal photographer.

Each of the 16 countries taking part in the omnibus will release six stamps—four singles, (in sheets of 50) and two contained in a miniature sheet. The following United Kingdom Overseas Territories are taking part: Ascension Island, Bermuda, British Antarctic Territory, British Indian Ocean Territory, Cayman Islands, Pitcairn Islands, Solomon Islands, St Helena, South Georgia and South Sandwich Islands and Tristan da Cunha. The other Commonwealth countries taking part in the omnibus are: Bahamas, Fiji, Kiribati, Samoa, Tokelau, and Vanuatu.

Her Majesty Queen Elizabeth 11 was born on 21 April 1926, at 17 Bruton Street, Mayfair, the London home of her parents the Duke and Duchess of York, the future King George VI and Queen Elizabeth. The infant princess was christened

The Queen's 80th birthday is celebrated by a series of formal and informal portraits

Royal Approval

The stamps issued by the United Kingdom Overseas Territories need formal Royal Approval, which they are allowed to signify by use of the Queen's Head or Royal Cypher. As a matter of courtesy, and as the Royal Coat of Arms is depicted on each of them, all the other stamps and souvenir sheets were shown to The Queen, who acknowledged them. The souvenir sheets, and single stamps, were designed by the CASB Studios and printed by BDT International Security Printers in Dublin, using the lithography process.

> The stamps depict formal and informal portraits

Die proofs of different engraved heads by Bradbury Wilkinson used on the first stamps of The Queen's reign

Right: Hand-painted essay in blue and chinese white of Bechuanaland 3d. Royal Visit stamp issued in 1947 and depicting the Princesses Margaret and Elizabeth. The portrait of Princess Elizabeth has been used for the 100v. stamp of Vanuatu in the 80th birthday omnibus (top right)

Essay and die proof from the Crown Agents archive, provided courtesy of the British Library

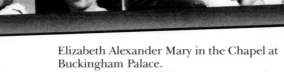

The young Princess

Corgis are The Queen's favourite dogs

Elizabeth Alexander Mary in the Chapel at Buckingham Palace.

Beautiful shots of the very young princess are shown on the Cayman Islands 15c., British Antarctic Territory 45p, Ascension Island 20p, Samoa $1, and Tristan da Cunha 60p stamps.

Princess Elizabeth was educated at home with her sister Princess Margaret. She was a keen horsewoman in her childhood and has remained so all her life. Princess Elizabeth also enjoyed amateur dramatics, was a good swimmer and became a girl guide before eventually becoming a sea ranger. The Queen is depicted in her teens on the St Helena 10p, Fiji 50c. and Kiribati 50c. stamps.

Favourite dogs

The Queen is featured with her favourite dogs, Corgis, on the Bermuda 35c., and South Georgia 50p stamps. The Queen has owned more than 30 Corgis during her reign, starting with Susan whom she received as an 18th birthday present in 1944. The Royal Corgi relationship started in 1933 when the then Duke of York, later to become King George VI, presented a Corgi, Dookie, to his two young Princesses, Elizabeth and Margaret.

When the Queen was 16 she was made Colonel in Chief of the Grenadier Guards. During the Second World War she joined the Auxiliary Territorial Service, at the Camberley Mechanical Transport Training Centre, working on vehicle maintenance. The Queen is shown in her khaki uniform on the Vanuatu 50v. and British Indian Ocean Territory 26p stamps.

In October 1940 The Queen made her first broadcast through the BBC to the children of the Commonwealth. She has made a Christmas broadcast to the Commonwealth every year of her reign except 1969, when a repeat of the film *Royal Family* was shown and a written message from The Queen issued.

The teenage Princess (above) and in the uniform of the Auxiliary Transport Service (below)

The Queen has owned more than 30 Corgis during her reign

The 80th Birthday of HM Queen Elizabeth II

Garter ceremony and Trooping the Colour

The Queen celebrates two birthdays each year—her personal birthday on 21 April and her Official Birthday, on the second or third Saturday in June

The omnibus includes a wide selection of both formal and informal portraits of The Queen, including a magnificent portrait of her at a Garter Ceremony on the Fiji $2 and Ascension Island £1 values. The Order of the Garter dates back to 1348 and is now over 650 years old, the oldest surviving order of chivalry in the world. Appointments to the Garter are made personally by The Queen.

Trooping the Colour
The Queen celebrates two birthdays each year—her personal birthday on 21 April and her Official Birthday, on the second or third Saturday in June. Trooping the Colour takes place on The Queen's official birthday when the colour of a Foot Guard's battalion is trooped before the Sovereign.

The Queen has been at the saluting base of her troops in every Trooping the Colour ceremony since the start of her reign, with the exception of 1955, when a national rail strike forced the cancellation of the parade.

The Queen took the parade on horseback until 1986 and wore a splendid scarlet uniform and tricorn hat. She is shown in this uniform on the 40c. Cayman Islands stamp and is depicted with Prince Charles just after the parade on the Samoa $1.75 stamp.

The Queen became the fifth-longest serving British monarch on 21 June 2002. Only four other kings and queens in British history have had longer reigns. These are: Queen Victoria, 63 years; George III, 59 years; James VI of Scotland (I of England) 58 years, and Henry III, 56 years.

In 50 years The Queen has undertaken over 250 official overseas visits to 128 different countries. Many of her official tours were undertaken on the Royal Yacht *Britannia*. It was launched by Her Majesty on 16 April 1953 and was commissioned for service on 7 January 1954. It was de-

commissioned in December 1997. During this time, *Britannia* travelled more than a million miles on Royal and official duties. The Queen's official visits have ranged from the Cocos Islands, with a population of 655, to The People's Republic of China, 3.7 million square miles with a population of 1.25 billion.

First tour
The Queen's first Commonwealth tour began on 24 November 1953, and included visits to Canada, Bermuda, Jamaica, Panama, Fiji, Tonga, New Zealand, Australia, the Cocos Islands, Ceylon, Aden, Uganda, Libya, Malta and Gibraltar. The total distance covered was 43,618 miles.

Since 1952 The Queen has given Royal Assent to more than 3200 Acts of Parliament, and given regular Tuesday evening audiences to ten Prime Ministers. They are: Winston Churchill 1951–55, Sir Anthony Eden 1955–57, Harold Macmillan 1957–63, Sir Alec Douglas-Home 1963–64, Harold Wilson 1964–70 and 1974–76, Edward Heath 1970–74, James Callaghan 1976–79, Margaret Thatcher 1979–90, John Major 1990–97, and Tony Blair 1997 to the present day.

Nigel Fordham, former head of the Crown Agents Stamp Bureau, who acted as a consultant to the issue said: 'The 80th Birthday of Her Majesty The Queen is an astonishing milestone in what is a most successful and popular reign. The stamps produced in the Crown Agents omnibus have imaginatively captured the life of Her Majesty during the past 80 years.'

Tim Graham, the distinguished Royal Photographer, took 13 of the pictures depicted on the stamps included in this Birthday omnibus. They are: Ascension Island £1.30 and the £1 value in the miniature sheet (the right-hand stamp, showing the Queen smiling); British Indian

Ocean Territory £1.10; Bahamas 50c. and 65c.; Bermuda $1.25; Cayman Islands $2; Kiribati $2; St Helena 80p; Solomon Islands $5 and $20; Tristan da Cunha 60p (showing the Queen wearing sunglasses and looking to the right) and Vanuatu 200v.

Tim Graham has been photographing the Queen since the early 1970s. In an exclusive interview with *GSM* he said: 'During more than 30 years I have accompanied The Queen on official visits throughout the UK, to the USA, the Gulf States, India, Africa, the Far East, within Europe and to many Commonwealth countries.

'By invitation, I have photographed The Queen at home in Windsor Castle in a one to one session to produce a series of official photographs and a photograph to commemorate her Ruby Wedding Anniversary.'

The Queen married HRH The Prince Philip, Duke of Edinburgh, at Westminster Abbey on 20 November 1947.

Trepidation

When asked which was the most difficult photograph he had ever taken he replied: 'I faced with trepidation the prospect of photographing the eight reigning monarchs of Europe when they gathered at Windsor Castle to mark The Queen's Golden Jubilee in 2002.

'Dreading the prospect of having to direct Your Majesty and His Majesty and Her Majesty, I was relieved to find that, having had such photographs taken on countless occasions during their reigns, the monarchs needed very little directing.

'The historic photograph, which had been taken at The Queen's personal request, was only the second time in a hundred years that all the European monarchs had been pictured in such a portrait.'

Asked to identify his favourite photograph featured in this omnibus, Tim Graham opted for the image of the Queen taking a photograph with her own camera. He pointed out: 'It might surprise some people to know that The Queen is a very keen amateur photographer. Having been on the other side of the lens for so many thousands of images taken in this country and overseas she has herself compiled an album of souvenir photographs from her travels throughout the world.'

When asked if he had been able to pass on any camera tips Tim shook his head.

Tim Graham revealed that his father had been an avid stamp collector over many years and, while recognising that his travels would have given him a perfect opportunity to compile his own stamp collection, Tim hasn't yet adopted stamp collecting as a hobby. 'Keeping track of my thousands of photographs is enough of a hobby for me these days', he added with a characteristic smile.

The Queen is a keen amateur photographer—Tim Graham's favourite stamp in the series

The Royal Collection

www.jerseystamps.com
T: +44 (0)1534 516320, F: +44 (0)1534 516330
E: stamps@jerseypost.com

Jersey Post

2002 - Royal Golden Jubilee of HM Queen Elizabeth II, 1952-2002

First Day Cover envelope

Spend £20 or more on the Royal Collection, quoting Ref. GRC10, and receive a limited edition Miniature Sheet featuring The Queen Mother **Absolutely Free!**

First Wedding Anniversary of HRH The Prince of Wales & HRH The Duchess of Cornwall - 2006

FDC & Pack

2008 - 60th Birthday of HRH The Prince of Wales

FDC & Pack

Souvenir Mini Sheet (SMS), FDC & Pack

2006 - 80th Birthday of Her Majesty Queen Elizabeth II

FDC & Pack

40th Anniversary Investiture HRH The Prince of Wales 2009

Miniature Sheet (M/S)

FDC & Pack

2007 - Royal Diamond Wedding Anniversary

FDC & Pack

Look out for Jersey's - 85th Birthday of HM The Queen *and* Royal Wedding stamps to be issued in 2011!

Enter Mint or CTO quantity:

	Mint	CTO	Total £
2002 Golden Jubilee Stamp £3			
Golden Jubilee Sheet of 4 Stamps £12			
Golden Jubilee Stamp FDC £3.75			
2006 1st Wedding Anniversary Stamp £2			
1st Wedding Anniversary Sheet of 4 Stamps £8			
1st Wedding Anniversary FDC £2.80			
1st Wedding Anniversary Pack £2.80			
2006 HM Queen 80th Birthday Stamp £5			
HM Queen 80th Birthday Sheet of 4 Stamps £20			
HM Queen 80th Birthday FDC £5.80			
HM Queen 80th Birthday Pack £5.80			
2007 Royal Diamond Wedding Stamp £3			
Royal Diamond Wedding Sheet of 4 Stamps £12			
Royal Diamond Wedding FDC £3.85			
Royal Diamond Wedding Pack £3.85			
2008 HRH Prince of Wales 60th Stamp £4			
HRH Prince of Wales 60th Sheet of 4 Stamps £16			
HRH Prince of Wales 60th FDC Stamp £4.90			
HRH Prince of Wales 60th Pack Stamp £4.90			
HRH Prince of Wales 60th Souv Mini Sheet £4			
HRH Prince of Wales 60th SMS FDC £4.90			
HRH Prince of Wales 60th SMS Pack £4.90			
2009 Investiture 40th Anniversary M/S £3			
Investiture 40th Anniversary M/S FDC £3.95			
Investiture 40th Anniversary M/S Pack £3.95			
Yes, I have spent over £20 - please send my free Queen Mother limited edition Mini Sheet (tick the box)			*free*

Please ensure you add the correct postage to each separate order form: UK - £1.85, Europe £2.00, Rest of World £3.00.

GRC10 TOTAL £

Orders are subject to availability. Should stocks of The Queen Mother Miniature Sheet become exhausted, an alternative product will be sent.

Photocopies are acceptable

Please send your completed form to:-
Jersey Philatelic Bureau, POHQ, JERSEY JE1 1AB
Please note if P&P fee is incorrect we cannot process the order.

Jersey Philatelic Account no. (if applic.)

Please use BLOCK LETTERS
Mr/Mrs/Miss/Other _____ Initial(s)_____
Surname _____
Address _____
_____
_____ Postcode _____
VAT no. (if applic.)_____
I enclose a payment of £ _____ (cheques payable to Jersey Post Ltd)
☐ Or charge my Jersey Philatelic Account number detailed above. (Tick box)
Or charge my Mastercard/Visa/Maestro/Delta number:

American Express and Diners Club are no longer accepted.

Expiry date _____ Valid from _____ Issue no. _____

Signature _____ Date _____

Royal Wedding Stamps Postponed as Prince Charles Attends Funeral of Pope John Paul II in Rome

'HRH The Prince of Wales and Mrs Parker Bowles are delighted with the stamps' Paddy Harverson, Communications Secretary to HRH The Prince of Wales tells Peter Jennings FRPSL, FRGS

The Royal Wedding between HRH The Prince of Wales and Mrs Parker Bowles was postponed for a day to allow Prince Charles to attend the Funeral of Pope John Paul II in Rome as representative of The Queen.

Royal Mail announced on Tuesday 5 April that it was: 'postponing the launch of its Royal Wedding stamps for 24 hours until Saturday 9 April'.

The 30p first class stamp depicts the couple in an informal and relaxed mood, enjoying the Mey Highland Games at Castle Mey, near John O'Groats during August 2004. The cost of sending a first class letter increased from 28p to 30p on 7 April 2005. The 68p stamp, the price of posting a letter abroad, shows Prince Charles and Mrs Parker Bowles pictured together at Birkhall, the Prince's Scottish residence on The Queen's Balmoral estate in Scotland during January this year.

These stamps were not sold individually but as a miniature sheet—containing two 30p and two 68p stamps, price £1.96—that includes the wording in English and Welsh: '8 APRIL HRH THE PRICE OF WALES AND MRS CAMILLA PARKER BOWLES'. A presentation pack was also available, price £2.50, but no stamp cards were produced for this issue.

The Royal Mail announcement on 5 April continued: 'The date on the miniature sheet stamps will remain as Friday 8 April but the stamps will not be available to buy until Saturday, the postponed wedding day of The Prince of Wales and Mrs Camilla Parker Bowles.'

Royal Mail's Head of Special Stamps, Julietta Edgar, said: 'In response to the announcement that the Royal Wedding has been postponed it is only right that we issue the stamps a day later than planned.'

Royal Mail added: 'The Windsor souvenir postmark will also be made available on 9 April and the stamps will be on sale for 12 months.' The heir to the throne and Mrs Parker Bowles had planned to marry in a civil ceremony at Windsor Guildhall Register Office, during the afternoon of Friday 8 April.

Clarence House announced on Monday 4 April, that following the death of the 84-year-old Polish Pope at the Vatican on Saturday evening, 2 April, the couple would postpone their wedding until Saturday 9 April as a mark of respect. The Prime Minster, Tony Blair, also delayed naming the date of the general election—Thursday 5 May—for 24 hours.

Pre-cancelled first day covers

Large numbers of Royal Mail covers, as well as those produced by a range of cover dealers, had already been pre-cancelled with the date 8 April. Patrick O'Neill, Head of Commercial PR, Group Communications at Royal Mail, told me: 'Stamp collectors who want the Royal Mail first day cover cancelled with the special Windsor souvenir postmark on the actual Wedding Day itself, Saturday 9 April, may order it from Royal Mail Tallents House in Edinburgh'. Collectors can submit their own covers for the First Day of Issue postmarks not later than 5 May 2005 to any of Royal Mail's five Special Handstamp Centres—London, Birmingham, South Shields, Cardiff or Glasgow.

The irony is that if Royal Mail had issued two individual stamps to commemorate the Royal Wedding rather than a miniature sheet there would not have been a problem with the date. Hugh Jefferies, Stanley Gibbons Catalogue Editor, said: 'I am sorry that it has been felt necessary to issue these stamps only in miniature sheet form as these will inevitably have limited short-term availability at post offices.'

Jefferies added: 'Important royal celebrations such as the marriage of the Prince of Wales should be reflected in widespread use of the special stamps. They should not be limited to souvenir items, most of which will be stored away in stamp albums and never see the inside of a postbox.'

Little option

Having distributed supplies of the Royal Wedding miniature sheet to a network of more than 15,000 Post Office branches throughout the United Kingdom, Royal Mail was left with little option but to put them on sale on the day of the wedding. It would have been a logistical nightmare to recall the miniature sheets, presentation packs, and pre-cancelled first day covers dated 8 April. Royal Mail Key Account holders would have been extremely reluctant to hand supplies back as stamp collectors worldwide scrambled to get hold of a miniature sheet dated 8 April.

Another logistical problem that faced stamp collectors and non-collectors alike was the fact that many post offices close at 1.00 p.m. on a Saturday. According to Royal Mail, post offices in Windsor have a range of opening hours on Saturdays—from 8.30 a.m. to 1.00 p.m., and 9.00 a.m to 4.00 p.m. Nationally, post office branch closing times on Saturday afternoons vary between 12.30 p.m. and 5.00 p.m.

Buckingham Palace Press Office would not confirm the date that the stamps received Royal Approval from The Queen, but I believe that it took place on Tuesday 8 March. Later that day information and an image of the miniature sheet were given to Press Association, under embargo.

Royal Mail finally unveiled the two stamps on Wednesday 9 March and I emailed the following questions to Clarence House Press Office: 'What is the reaction of HRH The Prince of Wales and Mrs Camilla Parker Bowles to the Royal Mail stamps? On what date did they select the photographs? Would they like the Crown Agents Stamp Bureau to issue Royal Wedding stamps on behalf of the Overseas Territories?'

'Delighted'

Within half an hour I received the following response from Paddy Harverson, Communications Secretary to HRH The Prince of Wales: 'HRH The Prince of Wales and Mrs Parker Bowles are delighted with the stamps. The photographs were approved by them via this office. I don't know the exact date, but it was last week. After their approval, the stamps then needed to be submitted to Buckingham Palace for the final go-ahead.'

Mr Harverson added: 'If more territories wished to issue stamps, I am sure HRH The Prince of Wales and Mrs Parker

• •

If Royal Mail had issued two individual stamps to commemorate the Royal Wedding rather than a miniature sheet there would not have been a problem

Bowles, and Buckingham Palace, would be happy to consider any such requests. But I would not want to pre-judge any final decision.'

The picture of Prince Charles and Mrs Parker Bowles on the 30p stamp was taken by Christopher Furlong, a former *Birmingham Evening Mail* photographer, from Walsall in the West Midlands, now working for Getty Images agency in Glasgow. Furlong was quoted in the *Evening Mail* on 10 March: 'The first I knew about my photo appearing on a stamp was when I

saw it in the papers in Scotland yesterday. I am absolutely delighted.'

The picture used on the 68p stamp was taken by Carolyn Robb, one of Britain's leading organic chefs, who told a Sunday newspaper that the image had been used without consent. She explained that she had been asked to take the picture at Birkhall during the couple's stay in January. 'I was told they wanted a photograph of themselves dressed in their new green tweeds. I often carried a camera to take pictures of food that I had prepared.'

The Times reported on 14 March that: 'Ms Robb claimed she was shocked to see the photograph flashed around the world as an official engagement picture, which also appears on a stamp to commemorate the royal wedding.'

Other issues?

On Tuesday 5 April I spoke to Dot Tilbury, Manager, Philatelic Bureau, Isle of Man Post, who said: 'We have no plans to issue any stamps to celebrate the Royal Wedding of The Prince of Wales and Camilla Parker Bowles.' The message from Andrée Valentine, Head of Philatelic Services, Jersey Post, was the same. She said: 'Jersey Post has no plans to issue a special set of stamps for the Royal Wedding on 9 April.'

Jeff Scott, Director of the Crown Agents Stamp Bureau told me: 'Crown Agents Stamp Bureau has been working with two of its clients towards the production of commemorative stamps for this occasion. It has never been our intention to produce an issue to be available for the actual date of the wedding—we have always proposed releasing the stamps some time afterwards. This will allow us, we hope, to incorporate designs which will reflect, amongst others, images of the royal couple on the wedding day itself, and actually as husband and wife.'

Mr Scott added: 'To this extent, the change to the date of the wedding has had no impact on our plans. Any necessary amendments to time and date to appear on the issues, together with any descriptive narrative, can easily be accommodated.'

Presentation pack, first day postmarks and miniature sheet

We have catalogues to suit every aspect of stamp collecting

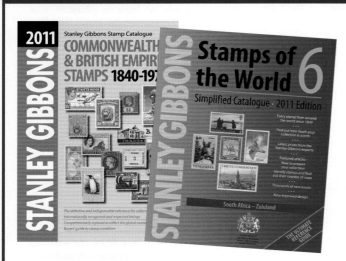

Our catalogues cover stamps issued from across the globe - from the Penny Black to the latest issues. Whether you're a specialist in a certain reign or a thematic collector, we should have something to suit your needs. All catalogues include the famous SG numbering system, making it as easy as possible to find the stamp you're looking for.

Catalogues published by Stanley Gibbons include:

1 Commonwealth & British Empire Stamps 1840–1970
(113th edition, 2011)

Stamps of the World 2011
Volume 1   A–Chil
Volume 2   Chin–Geo
Volume 3   Ger–Ja
Volume 4   Je–New R
Volume 5   New S–Sor
Volume 6   Sou–Z

Commonwealth Country Catalogues

Australia and Dependencies
(6th edition, 2010)
Bangladesh, Pakistan & Sri Lanka
(1st edition, 2004)
Belize, Guyana, Trinidad & Tobago
(1st edition, 2009)
Brunei, Malaysia & Singapore
(3rd edition, 2009)

Canada (3rd edition, 2008)
Central Africa (2nd edition, 2008)
Cyprus, Gibraltar & Malta
(2nd edition, 2008)
East Africa with Egypt and Sudan
(2nd edition, 2008)
Eastern Pacific (1st edition, 2007)
Falkland Islands (4th edition, 2010)
Hong Kong (3rd edition, 2010)

India (including Convention and Feudatory States)
(3rd edition, 2009)
Indian Ocean (1st edition, 2006)
Ireland (4th edition, 2008)
Leeward Islands (1st edition, 2007)
New Zealand (4th edition, 2010)
Northern Caribbean, Bahamas & Bermuda (2nd edition, 2009)

St. Helena & Dependencies
(3rd edition, 2007)
Southern Africa (2nd edition, 2007)
West Africa (1st edition, 2009)
Western Pacific (2nd edition, 2009)
Windward Islands and Barbados
(1st edition, 2007)

Foreign Countries

2 **Austria & Hungary**
(7th edition, 2009)
3 **Balkans** (5th edition, 2009)
4 **Benelux** (6th edition, 2010)
5 **Czechoslovakia & Poland**
(6th edition, 2002)
6 **France** (7th edition, 2010)

7 **Germany** (8th edition, 2007)
8 **Italy & Switzerland**
(7th edition, 2010)
9 **Portugal & Spain** (5th edition, 2004)
10 **Russia** (6th edition, 2008)
11 **Scandinavia** (6th edition, 2008)
12 **Africa since Independence A-E**

(2nd edition, 1983)
13 **Africa since Independence F-M**
(1st edition, 1981)
14 **Africa since Independence N-Z**
(1st edition, 1981)
15 **Central America** (3rd edition, 2007)
16 **Central Asia** (4th edition, 2006)

17 **China** (7th edition, 2006)
18 **Japan & Korea** (5th edition, 2008)
19 **Middle East** (7th edition, 2009)
20 **South America** (4th edition, 2008)
21 **South-East Asia** (4th edition, 2004)

Great Britain Catalogues

Collect British Stamps
(61st edition, 2010)
Great Britain Concise Stamp Catalogue
(25th edition, 2010)

Volume 1   **Queen Victoria**
(15th edition, 2008)
Volume 2   **King Edward VII to King George VI**
(13th edition, 2009)
Volume 3   **Queen Elizabeth II Pre-decimal issues**
(11th edition, 2006)

Volume 4   **Queen Elizabeth II Decimal Definitive Issues – Part 1**
(10th edition, 2008)
Queen Elizabeth II Decimal Definitive Issues – Part 2
(10th edition, 2010)

Volume 5   **Queen Elizabeth II Decimal Special Issues**
(3rd edition, 1998 with 1998 99 and 2000/1 Supplements)

Thematic Catalogues

Stanley Gibbons Catalogues for use with **Stamps of the World.**
Collect Aircraft on Stamps
(2nd edition, 2009)
Collect Birds on Stamps
(5th edition, 2003)
Collect Chess on Stamps
(2nd edition, 1999)

Collect Fish on Stamps
(1st edition, 1999)
Collect Motor Vehicles on Stamps
(1st edition 2004)

Other publications
Philatelic Terms Illustrated
(4th edition, 2003)
How to Identify Stamps
(4th edition, 2007)

Collect Channel Islands and Isle of Man Stamps
(26th edition, 2010)
Great Britain Numbers Issued
(3rd edition, 2008)
Enjoy Stamp Collecting
(7th edition, 2006)
Antarctica (including Australian and British Antarctic Territories, French Southern and Antarctic

Territories and Ross Dependency)
(1st edition, 2010)
United Nations (also including International Organizations based in Switzerland and UNESCO)
(1st edition, 2010)

Stanley Gibbons Publications
7 Parkside, Christchurch Road, Ringwood, Hampshire BH24 3SH
UK: 0800 611 622 Int: +44 1425 363 | order@stanleygibbons.co.uk
www.stanleygibbons.com

Crown Agents 50th Anniversary of the Coronation Omnibus

This month's *Gibbons Stamp Monthly* comes with a free souvenir sheet, specially designed by the Crown Agents Stamp Bureau to accompany the forthcoming omnibus stamp series to celebrate the 50th anniversary of Her Majesty The Queen's Coronation. Hugh Jefferies visited the CASB in Sutton to see the work in progress and talked to Production Co-ordinator Graham Tapp about the work involved in organising an issue of this type

Hugh Jefferies: Well Graham, the Crown Agents have been producing omnibus issues for nearly 70 years now. With that level of experience and expertise, surely the design and production process must by now be fairly straightforward.
Graham Tapp: Yes, to an extent that's true. But a lot has changed over the past 70 years.
How do you mean?
Well, in 1935 the Crown Agents were organising stamp production for over 60 countries: nowadays the total is somewhat less.
I noticed you used the word 'organising' then. Wouldn't masterminding have been more apt?
No, definitely not. Not in the controlling

sense of the word. The Crown Agents Stamp Bureau have never dictated to their Principals. Recommendations are regularly made, some very positively. But the final decision always rests with the Principal.
You've hinted there that some administrations have decided not to participate in the latest omnibus that I believe is in the offing i.e. 50th Anniversary of the Coronation of Her Majesty Queen Elizabeth II. Is that for political reasons?
No. Many of those former colonies have gained independence since 1935 and their governments therefore strongly influence how, and if, they wish to honour or celebrate the 50th Anniversary of the Coronation of HM The Queen or other famous persons. So you can expect several other individual Coronation releases in addition to the Crown Agents' omnibus.
Which countries are participating in the Crown Agents Stamp Bureau's omnibus?
Ascension, Bahamas, Bermuda, British Antarctic Territory, British Indian Ocean Territory, British Virgin Islands, Cayman Islands, Jamaica, Kiribati, Pitcairn Islands, St Helena, St Lucia, Tokelau and Tristan da Cunha.

Who considers the various options/strategies for a stamp issue?
The Crown Agents Stamp Bureau has been at the heart of stamp collecting and the philatelic trade for many years. It is a lively scene almost impossible to even monitor from remote distances. Taking this into consideration, the Bureau prepares proposals continuously every year.

When members of the Royal Family are involved, e.g. Royal visits, significant birthdays and anniversaries—the initial proposals are submitted to Her Majesty for consideration. In fact, The Queen examines all stamp designs which bear her head or the Royal Cipher long before production commences.
It sounds to me from this, that any set of stamps can take up to six or eight months to contemplate, consider and produce.
Some take even longer, particularly new definitive sets numbering 12 to 16 values, but others can be a lot quicker.
Once a project is approved by Buckingham Palace, what is the next step?
Each potential overseas participant in an omnibus is then given a complete textual synopsis of design ideas, marketing strategies, special promotions, etc. Hopefully the postal administrations will respond promptly to these submissions.
Don't they?
Not always: it's not that easy for them.

Two of Andrew Robinson's 'free-form' designs (reduced to 75%)

Her Majesty Queen Elizabeth II's
Coronation

photographic image in order to sustain contiguity within the omnibus issue. Stamps must necessarily incorporate the central image, the monetary denomination, the country's name and also, for UK Overseas Territories, the Queen's head or Royal Cipher. There's not a lot of space on a stamp to do all that distinctly when you think about it.

I must admit, I hadn't thought about that before.

It is quite easy to cope with countries with short names, such as Bermuda, Jamaica or Tokelau, but it gets tricky when you have to fit in British Virgin Islands, Tristan da Cunha or British Indian Ocean Territory.

Why not?

Well, Postmasters General are responsible for running their countries' postal operations and services and may not have the unilateral power to accept, or refuse, the Crown Agents' recommendations. They, in turn, need to consult with members of their Stamp Advisory Committee (or similar official body with analogous name and responsibilities), their respective Minister and, sometimes, the entire Cabinet of Ministers.

The process seems to get lengthier and lengthier.

I suppose so but, in fact, modern communication facilities do speed matters up considerably. With email technology, work can be conducted very quickly.

OK. So the eventual participants signify that they will happily join in. What then?

Decisions have to be taken by the Crown Agents Stamp Bureau as to what sort of artwork will be needed and which designers should be invited to submit examples or speculative treatments.

How do you mean 'what sort of artwork'?

Well, the subject could best be represented by portraiture, or landscape views, or natural history, etc. Designers usually specialise in particular styles and disciplines.

What style did the Bureau recommend for the Coronation omnibus?

Genuine photographs, both for the main stamp images and the miniature sheet surrounds.

That sounds easy: nobody could argue against genuine photos of actual events.

That's true. However, modern stamps are almost always multicoloured, whereas colour photography was not all that common in 1953.

Furthermore, although 'candid' camera shots taken through telescopic lenses are fine for national newspapers and magazines, the focusing is, more often than not, short of the standards required for postage stamp design and printing.

I suppose not.

It doesn't end there. We require high resolution photographs, not simply to create a clear image when reduced several percentages (to stamp size), but also,

because fine-screen printing techniques would only blur a poor quality photograph, if used, even further. So, for the Coronation omnibus we had to sort through hundreds of photographs from several internationally renowned photographic agencies before reaching the final selections.

Any other problems?

One, which we quickly solved was how to create similar borders for each

Now that you've shown them to me, it is apparent that the Omnibus items are all in a familiar, perhaps I should say 'traditional' format, i.e. rectangular. Was there a deliberate attempt to retain a link with the 1953 style or did you try some other experiments?

We have been aware, for quite some time, that innovations in stamp production have gone way beyond the

Above: Alternative proposals suggested by Andrew Robinson (reduced to 75%) Right: Imperforate colour proof of the Tristan da Cunha miniature sheet Centre: Imperforate running proof of the St Helena stamps and miniature sheet Far right: The issued set and miniature sheet for Pitcairn Islands

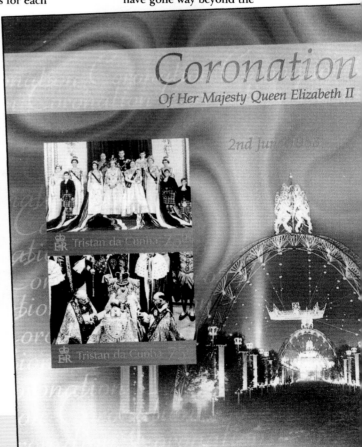

experimental stages. Royal Mail released a set of self-adhesive, free-form, stamps dubbed 'Fun fruit & veg' on 25 March. These are of irregular shape and a separate sheet of 76 stickers is available which gives users (probably mainly youngsters) the opportunity to make up private cartoons with the stamps before posting cards and letters to their friends.

Andrew Robinson, who prepared the overall format of the omnibus set for us, tried out several free-form design ideas.

However, the Coronation, whilst bringing a lot of enjoyment and excitement to the people of Britain and the Commonwealth, is of solemn, dignified, historical importance. Britain's commemoratives of the 50th Anniversary will not be cartoon-like and, consequently, Andrew's free-shaped submissions were not adopted. They weren't wrong but, somehow, they didn't seem right. They didn't fit in with the occasion.

Clearly, devising and designing an issue of this type is a somewhat more complex task than we collectors imagine. Are there any other problems to overcome?

Well, my computer records that since January I have sent over 500 email messages to our overseas clients regarding the Coronation omnibus. In addition, there have been dozens of phone calls because, as I mentioned earlier, the

Crown Agents Stamp Bureau works in constant co-operation with their overseas Principals.

Not only must stamps be produced to the highest standards—in this case by De La Rue Global Services, Byfleet, Surrey—but delivered on time to far-away places like Pitcairn Islands and St Helena. Neither of these have airstrips but rely upon none-too-frequent shipping opportunities. All this, and much more, demands critical co-ordination.

We certainly hope that our efforts have been worthwhile and that the omnibus proves popular with the general public and stamps collectors throughout the world.

Images on the stamps and sheetlets include Her Majesty travelling from Buckingham Palace to Westminster Abbey before the Coronation: this appears on the Pitcairn Islands miniature sheet. Early preparations feature on a Jamaica stamp. Then comes the ceremony itself (Cayman Islands) and, afterwards, the Royal Family assembled on the balcony of Buckingham Palace to watch the flypast of Royal Air Force jet planes (British Virgin Islands). The Queen and Duke of Edinburgh wave happily back (Kiribati) to the thousands of jubilant spectators who stayed in The Mall (specially festooned with colourful illuminations) long into the night (Tristan da Cunha miniature sheet).

Thank you very much for talking to me so thoroughly.

It's been a pleasure.

Overleaf: Prince William's 21st birthday

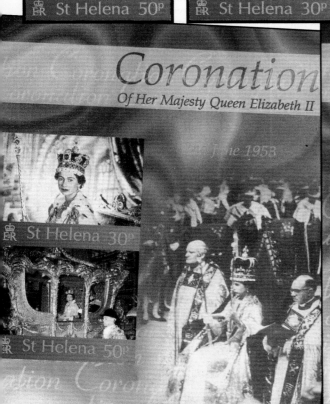

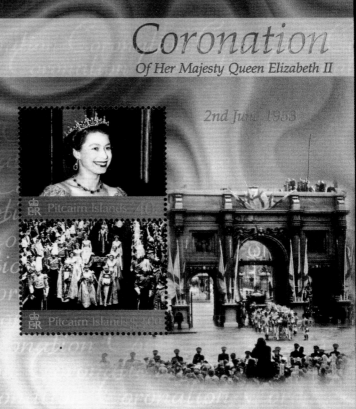

21st Birthday of Prince William of Wales

News has been released that the Crown Agents Stamp Bureau will shortly be presenting a 'minibus' of stamps and sheetlets marking the 21st birthday of His Royal Highness Prince William of Wales, which occurs on 21 June.

Organising this project, whilst simultaneously co-ordinating the omnibus commemorating the 50th anniversary of the Coronation of Her Majesty Queen Elizabeth II, must have put quite a strain on the Crown Agents Stamp Bureau resources, yet it appears that all has run smoothly and according to plan.

Vicky Jones was the co-ordinator and she modestly remarks that her activities, and anxieties, were similar to Graham Tapp's, but less hectic because eight countries wished to participate. Even so, a vast amount of modern photographic material was available and had to be scrutinised and approved.

published in all the major picture magazines and newspapers around the globe and over the years his photographs have become one of the most comprehensive Royal archives of our time, called upon by researchers everywhere. Books, TV documentaries, websites, postcards, stamps, coins, calendars—even some of the Royal Family's Christmas cards—feature Tim's images.

Recognition of his excellent work led to invitations to photograph the Royal Family at home, pictures that would capture some of the most charming and relaxed family moments ever: wedding anniversary pictures of the Queen and Prince Philip, Prince Edward for his coming-of-age, Princess Michael and her children, Princess Alice, the Duke and Duchess of Gloucester and their family, and Lady Helen Windsor. Perhaps the pictures he is best known for are his captivating photographs of the Prince and Princess of Wales with their children.

His latest book, *William*, with the court correspondent Peter Archer, is a unique collection of Tim's favourite photographs of the Prince; from the first picture he took when the new Royal prince was just a day old, to the latest image of the Prince as very much a man of the moment.

No wonder his photographs have been chosen for the stamps that commemorate the Prince's 21st birthday.

Each participating country in the Crown Agents' minibus issue (Ascension, British Indian Ocean Territory, British Virgin Islands, Cayman Islands, Falkland Islands, South Georgia and the South Sandwich Islands, Tokelau and Tristan da Cunha) will release a sheetlet of ten stamps (five pairs) with a contemporary scene of Prince William at leisure, positioned vertically alongside.

British Virgin Islands will repeat its two stamps in separate sheets of 20, to distinguish them, they appear with a grey border, while Cayman Islands are issuing two additional values, also in sheets of 20.

Full details of each of the photographed occasions will be provided to purchasers of the minibus set and first day covers. Several lively shots of the Prince playing polo (proceeds to charities) contrast with a pensive expression as he prepares for admission to university. He is seen, with his father, Prince Charles, surveying the snowy terrain prior to skiing at Klosters, Switzerland, and strolling back to camp after a day's hard work repairing walkways in the rain forests of southern Chile.

He is seriously about to emulate David Beckham during an inter-house football match between Gailey's and Hurst's, Eton College, Windsor, on 16 June 2000, and smiling gently during Her Majesty The Queen Mother's 101st birthday party at Clarence House, London, on 4 August 2001.

Because not all post offices open on a Saturday, and for other practical/logistical reasons, the release dates for these sheetlets vary slightly over the period 20 to 23 June and individual cancellation cachets have, therefore, been produced for use on first day covers.

Now we'll just let the philatelic portraits speak for themselves.

'A Happy Birthday, your Highness!'

It was decided at the outset that, as a tributary omnibus was released to mark the Prince's 18th birthday (2000), this new commemoration should consist of up-to-date scenes. His Royal Highness is an exceedingly mobile and energetic young man and the images selected from Tim Graham's vast array of formal and informal portraits brings this point home very well. 'Every picture is worth a thousand words' as they say.

For 30 years, and in more than a hundred countries around the world, Tim Graham has recorded, with thousands of photographs, the lives of the Royal Family. His day-to-day coverage is

The Coronation and Beyond

John Woolford celebrates the 50th anniversary of Her Majesty's Coronation by recalling some of the philatelic highlights of her reign

Half a century ago—sadly, I remember it well!—the Coronation of Elizabeth II saw the issue of many new stamps in the British Commonwealth. In Southern Rhodesia where I lived (I was very young, I hasten to point out), 2 June, the day of the Coronation, was a public holiday—quite rightly—so there was no question of a new stamp coming out that day. After all, it would have been bad for business.

So the 2s.6d. Coronation stamp (SG 77) was issued on 1 June 1953. I recall clutching a half-crown, which was real money in those days, and standing in the queue at Umtali Post Office in search of the new stamps. From time to time my mother popped in to see if the queue was moving; and eventually I parted with my half-crown and stuck the new stamp on an envelope that my father had provided and addressed for me on the grounds that I would not be able to do it properly—he was probably right—and I have that first day cover still. The stamp is not rare, despite its high face value, and 290,658 were sold. It was not withdrawn until the end of July, although I believe it was sold out in Umtali before then.

The next excitement was the arrival in the ordinary post of a first day cover from a favourite uncle in England (who started me on this maddening hobby of philately that has taken over my life) bearing the Great Britain set. I was amused even then to note that in Britain they were behind the straight talking, straight shooting, no-nonsense colonials and did not have their stamps until the day after the Coronation, on 3 June.

No shortage of buyers

The various colonies issued a common design, and they seemed to stick to the correct date of 2 June. Northern Rhodesia and Nyasaland, soon to be joined with Southern Rhodesia in the Federation of Rhodesia and Nyasaland, had low value stamps in the omnibus design—1½d. for Northern Rhodesia and 2d. for Nyasaland. Both countries, like Southern Rhodesia, had already had stamps with the head of the new Queen—for the Rhodes Centenary Exhibition—and there was no shortage of buyers for the Coronation stamps:

almost 2 million of the Northern Rhodesia and over 1,300,000 of the Nyasaland stamps being sold.

South Africa had a splendid looking 2d. stamp, of which over 47 million were sold. South West Africa, although under the sway of a nominally anti-British government, had a most attractive set of five stamps with a top value of 1s. The face value of the lot was 2s.1d. There was a certain amount of speculation in these stamps as it was felt the 4d. in particular might be scarce. In the end it was shown that there were 248,760 of the 4d., 356,200 of the 1s. and 283,840 of the 6d., so there were no rarities in the set.

The Great Britain set was colourful enough, with four designers sharing the work, around a central portrait taken from a Dorothy Wilding photograph. The exception to the Dorothy Wilding portrait was the 1s.3d. stamp that was entirely the product of Edmund Dulac's imagination. This was used in a miniature sheet issued for the Stamp Show 2000 International in London. The Edmund Dulac design this time was adapted for the face value of £1, and the result was certainly striking.

Quiet charm

The stream of Coronation stamps of 1953 have never been as popular as, for example, the 1935 Silver Jubilee stamps, but they have a quiet charm. Nobody will make much from investing in them. Perhaps more fun can be had from hunting for the special Coronation 1953 airmail covers that were flown from England to Australia and other countries. They turn up from time to time, and are most attractive.

In the 1960s the 'first' definitives of many colonies were sought after by collectors and dealers. They were stamps, such as the Gibraltar 1953 set, SG 145/58, that were succeeded some years later by the 'second' definitives issued in 1960. Search the catalogue and you will find many such issues from Antigua to Zanzibar (although the latter country never had a set showing the head of Elizabeth II).

These 'first' definitives have done fairly well over the years since then. The Gibraltar set, with only 49 thousand of the 10s.

Colonial Omnibus issues from Northern Rhodesia and Nyasaland together with Coronation stamps from South Africa, South West Africa and Great Britain

First Elizabethan definitives from Gibraltar,
Falkland Islands and Falkland Islands
Dependencies

European collectors viewed the British habit of mounting mint stamps as insular barbarism

and 53 thousand of the £1 is still good property, especially unmounted mint. A set that was hunted with great determination as I recall was the Falkland Islands issue of 1955–57, SG 187/92, which was succeeded in 1960 by a long set up to £1, SG 193/207. The Falklands Dependencies definitives of 1954–62, SG G26/G40, attracted much attention as the work of the two printers, Waterlow and De La Rue, can be distinguished in some cases. The re-entries on the 1d. and 3d. were popular, and ought not to be ignored even now.

Bringing out the detail

Much attention was paid in the 1960s and 1970s to Elizabethan stamps of Cyprus, Gibraltar and Malta as it was thought demand in Europe would push prices higher. To some extent that happened, although not as much as was fondly imagined a generation ago. The Malta 1956 definitives, printed by Bradbury, Wilkinson (up to 2s.) and Waterlow (2s.6d. to £1) became extremely popular after their withdrawal in 1965 (the farthing remained on sale for another six years), and with the European demand for unmounted mint (for decades European collectors viewed the British habit of mounting mint stamps as insular barbarism) prices for the Malta 1956 set soon went through the roof. They have settled down somewhat now, but have never lost their popularity. Quantities sold were 198,139 of the £1, 199,143 of the 10s., 380,838 of the 5s., and rather more for the rest of them. The high values are particularly handsome, and the recess printing brought out the detail on each stamp very well.

The Cyprus 1955 definitives were recess printed by Bradbury, Wilkinson and a fine picture gallery they made. The top value 500 mils and £1 that showed coins and arms of different periods of the history of Cyprus were particularly attractive. Much fun was had with the 15 mils olive-green and indigo that was replaced by the slightly different yellow-olive and indigo stamp in

the middle of June 1960, just as the Independence set was about to be issued. The delay in the negotiations for the Independence of Cyprus led to the overprinted stamps being held back, and it is probable that it was thought the new printing of the 15 mils would not have to be issued. It is thought some were put on sale at the GPO in Nicosia on their arrival in April 1960, but the comparative rarity of such a low value stamp has given many collectors a lot of enjoyment—and why not?

The Independence overprints, issued on 16 August 1960, have been popular from the word go, although the sales figures of 197,900 for the £1 and over a quarter of a million for the 500 mils shows that they are not scarce.

Vanishing act

Much scarcer, and much hunted in central Africa, were the three 1953 definitive sets issued respectively by Southern Rhodesia, Northern Rhodesia, and Nyasaland in 1953. They were soon to be replaced by a new definitive set for the Federation of Rhodesia and Nyasaland (1 July 1954), and it was not long before they seemed to vanish from the market. The Southern Rhodesia £1, showing the Coat of Arms of the Colony, was one of the most impressive stamps of the period.

This Southern Rhodesia set was the most popular of the three, and was soon fetching £3 and then £5, either mint or used. The 2002 catalogue price of £60 mint and £70 used is lower than the £75 and £90 quoted in the *British Commonwealth Catalogue* that came out at the height of the speculative boom that caused such excitement in the 1970s.

The Nyasaland 1953 definitives were another handsome lot, with the designs based on those of the previous King George VI issue. Quantities of the top value £1 were just over 25,000, while there were 33,000 of the 10s., and 56,000 of the 5s. The 1981 catalogue prices were £24 mint and £35 used. In 2002 prices were £32 and £48 respectively. Try and find any of these stamps used in either Northern or Southern Rhodesia—they turn up from time to time, but are most unusual.

Northern Rhodesia's set of 1953 was apparently the most common of the three, with 30,000 of the £1 and 40,000 of the 10s. Again, the design was based on that of the earlier George VI set, and many collectors found it dull. The boom prices of 1981 were £29 mint and £48 used, and the 2002 prices £40 and £65.

A number of Elizabethan stamps had very short lives, and new issue services went to great trouble to obtain these supposed rarities. One stamp that was very

Malta's 1956 definitives were popular. The 1955
Cyprus issue is an attractive set and the
Independence overprint has also proved popular

Southern Rhodesia's £1
value was one of the
most impressive stamps
of the period

popular was the 10s. Sierra Leone, SG 22la, issued only a week or so before the 1961 definitives. The 2002 Catalogue price of £10 mint and £25 used shows that used (as is so often the case) have been under-appreciated. It is a difficult stamp, and a most attractive one.

Shame!

In Barbados the $2.40 with Block CA watermark caused a stir, as it was replaced just over a fortnight later by the new 'Marine Life' definitives. The short-lived $2.40 was bound to be a winner, thought the wiseacres; but probably too many dealers knew about it, as more than third of a century later its price stands at only £1.25 mint and £2 used. Shame! Somebody must have done a lot of buying back in 1965.

Perhaps the biggest disappointment was the Jamaica 8d. overprinted for Independence in 1962. In September 1963 the stamp appeared with the overprint at lower left (SG 187a). I remember visiting England when this stamp was 'discovered' so to speak, and my uncle, the very same uncle who had started me collecting stamps years before, told me with some glee that he had latched on to a couple of these overprint varieties from his new issue service, and one of them was for me. I think he had paid the vast sum of 7s.6d. for it. I was delighted. Today that stamp is priced at 15 pence, or three shillings!

Not all Elizabethan stamps were anti-climaxes. The various phosphor and phosphor-graphite issues of Great Britain were fascinating to watch from the wilds of Central Africa. Good old Uncle Henry saw that I kept up to date with them to the eventual profit of both of us. Some of them, I believe, came out of slot machines at Waterloo Station.

Caymans definitives adopted the then 'new' portrait of the Queen by Annigoni. Gilbert & Ellice Islands introduced a silhouette portrait, while Kenya, Uganda, and Tanganyika produced some rather 'ghostly' heads on their 1960 definitives. An interesting display of Elizabethan stamps can be assembled by concentrating on the different types of portrait, even without hunting for varieties. If that approach leads a beginner to true philately, so much the better!

In Rhodesia in the 1960s there was much excitement when various countries surcharged incoming letters that bore Rhodesian stamps. To accept such letters would upset those who made much display of not 'trading with the illegal regime'. Great fun was had by collectors, but many letters sent to Britain and franked with 'illegal' stamps were delivered normally. That was fair enough, as only a politician would be silly enough to gum up the works. Stamp dealers in Rhodesia did a large trade selling stamps that had the Queen's head on them, so that the purchasers could apply them to letters that would otherwise attract unwelcome attention.

Speculation

Inevitably, there was a lot of speculation in Rhodesian stamps of the period, and when it became possible for Gibbons to price Rhodesian stamps many remarkable valuations were quoted. Things have settled down, and many Rhodesian stamps of the 1960s have fallen from their dizzy heights. Those who wish to study stamps and not just accumulate them could do worse than concentrate on the 1966 Rhopex miniature sheets (MS392). There were about 25,000 sheets of each of the two printings, the second printing being on white paper. Of this total about 4166 'A' sheets exist, or

He had paid the vast sum of 7s.6d. for it. I was delighted. Today that stamp is priced at 15 pence

---

There was one Elizabethan set that was not a flop, and that was the Bahamas 1970 definitives on 'whiter' paper (SG 295a/ 309a). In the 2002 British Commonwealth Catalogue they were priced £450 mint and £250 used. Sadly, my interest in hunting for new issues had expired by then, and I never got them. The Bahamas has had many attractive definitives, and standards were not allowed to sink in the new reign. Still, the white paper stamps of 1970 are very difficult to find, as apparently only 1220 of the $3 and another 1220 of the $2 were sold. Now that is scarce.

Ghostly heads

Many Elizabethan issues, such as those from Bahamas, followed the example of many George VI stamps by providing a guided tour of the territory and its natural resources. One of the most colourful was the issue from Cayman Islands in 1953–59, and the later issue of 1962. The 1962

2083 of the first and 2083 of the second printing. These 'A' sheets can be identified by not having any perforations through the top margin, and only two holes extending from the horizontal rows into the left margin.

A worthwhile study can be made of some of the other Rhodesian issues that appeared during the UDI years 1965–80, and many notable collections of them exist already. However, a new generation has grown up since then, and there is no harm in taking a fresh look. After all, there can never be any more of them.

Discrimination is a dirty word now, but any collector who is discriminating can find a subject to engross him in the many Elizabethan stamps that have turned up in the last half century. Seek the genuinely scarce and the genuinely interesting, and don't throw your money away on a lot of common stamps, and you will have great fun.

Issues from Nyasaland, Northern Rhodesia, Sierra Leone, Barbados, Jamaica, Bahamas and Cayman Islands. Some had very short lives, though were not always a good investment

Philatelic Monarchy

David Green looks back at some of Guernsey Post's recent 'Royal' issues, including the free gift presented with this month's Gibbons Stamp Monthly

Perpetually striving to shake off its bookish image, stamp collecting has changed considerably in recent years. While there is still a core market of earnest collectors with specialised interests, the idea of having a little fun at the same time has steadily infiltrated the hobby.

The short time span since 1969, when Guernsey Post gained its independence from Royal Mail, makes stamps from this isle very attractive from a collector's point of view. It offers the chance to acquire a complete collection quite easily. Unsurprisingly too, there is a huge body of collectors who want anything with a majestic head on it. These are among that group known as thematic collectors, to whom the country of origin is of little importance—it's what is in the picture that counts.

Guernsey Post has certainly worked hard to provide the Royal thematic collector with an outstanding selection of quality issues. In recent years we've been treated to anniversaries, birthdays and even weddings of significant members of the Royal Household. But, typical of Guernsey and Alderney issues, it's never been over-done.

The free gift with this copy of *Gibbons Stamp Monthly* is with the compliments of Guernsey Post and sets the tone for an exceptional year of stamp design from Alderney and Guernsey. The dynamic miniature sheet from Alderney, entitled 'Long Live The Queen' shows the poignant moment when Princess Elizabeth set foot on British soil for the first time, as Sovereign.

'Bailiwick'—an explanation

'50 Glorious Years', a six-stamp set featuring the Queen's visit to the Bailiwick in 2001, was issued on 30 April 2002. It includes a superb prestige booklet with photographs of a sunny day in July, when it seemed the whole island flocked out to wave the customary 'Union Jack'. The set is filled with colourful, regal humanism. Unfortunately, it will be withdrawn from sale on 29 April. But, if you quote the reference 'Q5' or use the card with the free gift, those good people at the Guernsey Philatelic Bureau will honour orders until 15 May. (For those who are unsure of what 'Bailiwick' is, an explanation: a district under the jurisdiction of a bailiff. The 'Bailiwick' of Guernsey is the name given to the group of islands governed by Guernsey. These include Alderney, Sark and Herm, and the smaller, relatively unknown jewels: Brechou, Jethou and Lihou. The bailiff of Guernsey, appointed by the Crown, is the President of the legislative assembly and Royal Courts.)

The passing of HM The Queen Mother last year brought a wave of love across the British Isles and all over the world. A miniature sheet from Guernsey, issued on what would have been her 102nd birthday, was a fitting tribute to this remarkable woman, entitled 'Strength Dignity and Laughter'. The photographic portrait is complemented with a bouquet of white roses, sweet peas, freesias and mimosas which echoed the wreath laid by her daughter, Queen Elizabeth, on the day of the funeral. The

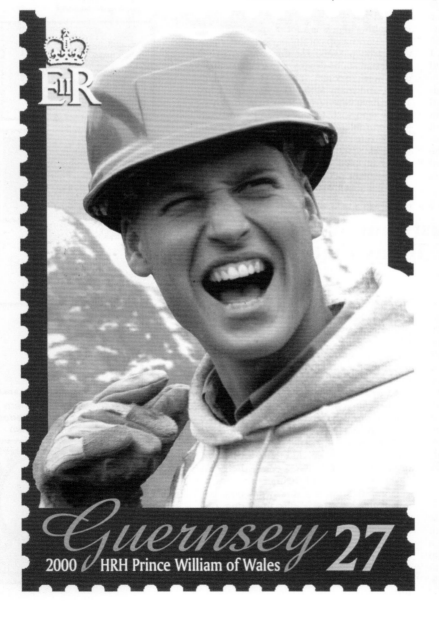

50 Glorious Years (bottom)

Strength Dignity and Laughter (right)

A Solemn Promise (below)

HRH Prince William of Wales 21st Birthday (left)

£2

BAILIWICK OF GUERNSEY

STRENGTH DIGNITY & LAUGHTER
HM QUEEN ELIZABETH THE QUEEN MOTHER
AUGUST 1900 – 30 MARCH 2002

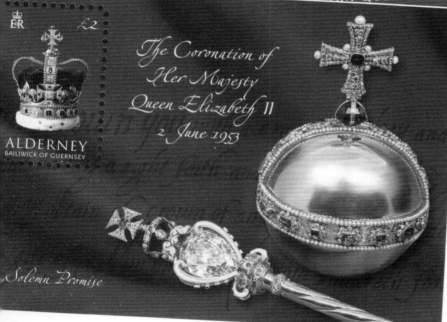

£2

The Coronation of
Her Majesty
Queen Elizabeth II
2 June 1953

ALDERNEY
BAILIWICK OF GUERNSEY

Solemn Promise

reath was later left on the tomb of the nknown soldier at Westminster Abbey, a adition the Queen Mother started herself n her wedding day. It's the finer details ke this that truly reflect Guernsey's accurte eye for detail and sheer sensitivity in very stamp issue produced.

Fitting treatment

The 50th anniversary of The Queen's Coronation, on 2 June, has been given a design treatment that the Guernsey Philatelic Bureau knows how to do very well indeed. The miniature sheet, entitled 'A Solemn Promise' features a stunning photograph of the Crown Jewels. The £2 stamp is the crown itself which has been blind embossed, a very fitting treatment for such a precious object.

Finally, an issue to definitely watch out for very soon commemorates the 21st birthday of HRH Prince William of Wales. This is the first time Prince William has ever appeared on a set from Guernsey. The ten stamps, in two strips of five, feature various stages of the royal prince's life. There is a stunning prestige booklet to accompany the set, which will surely entice young collectors into the world of stamp collecting.

Royal issues currently available from Guernsey Post:

50 Glorious Years
Set of six stamps, First Day Cover, Presentation Pack and Prestige Booklet

Strength Dignity and Laughter
Miniature Sheet, First Day Cover and Presentation Pack

A Solemn Promise
Miniature Sheet, First Day Cover and Presentation Pack
Coming soon:

HRH Prince William of Wales 21st Birthday
Set of ten stamps, First Day Cover, Presentation Pack and Prestige Booklet
Date of issue: 21 June 2003

If you would like further information on collecting stamps from Guernsey and Alderney, please write to us at:

Guernsey Philatelic Bureau
Envoy House
La Vrangue
St Peter Port
Guernsey
GY1 1AB

Tel: +44 (0) 1481 716486
Fax: +44 (0) 1481 712082
Email:
Philatelic@guernseypost.com
Website: www.guernseypost.com

1900-2002

30c $1·25

BERMUDA BERMUDA

Her Majesty Queen Elizabeth

The Queen Mother

The Crown Agents Stamp Bureau Pays Tribute to The Queen Mother

Peter Jennings FRPSL reviews the new Crown Agents omnibus celebrating the life of Queen Elizabeth The Queen Mother and discusses the series with its designer, Andrew Robinson

Her Majesty Queen Elizabeth The Queen Mother is depicted wearing an array of her famous hats on a special tribute in postage stamps and miniature sheets to mark her life, released world-wide on 5 August, the day after the 102nd anniversary of her birth.

Following The Queen Mother's death at Windsor on 30 March, the Crown Agents Stamp Bureau arranged a magnificent omnibus stamp issue on behalf of 17 countries including 11 United Kingdom Overseas Territories—Ascension, Bermuda, British Antarctic Territory, British Indian Ocean Territory, British Virgin Islands, Cayman Islands, Falkland Islands, Pitcairn Islands, St Helena, South Georgia and South Sandwich Islands, and Tristan da Cunha. The other countries, all members of the Commonwealth, taking part in this omnibus issue are—Bahamas, Nauru, Saint Lucia, Seychelles, Solomon Islands, and Tokelau.

There are 34 different images of The Queen Mother on the stamps and a fur-

ther 34 on the miniature sheets, making a wonderful collection of 68

The miniature sheet borders bear The Queen Mother's personal coat of arms as well as two different images from her life, either side of the stamps. All the stamps and miniature sheets have been printed on Crown Agents security watermarked paper by the House of Questa Limited. Selective embossing and varnishing has been used on the miniature sheet borders to highlight certain features of the design.

Microprinting

Beneath the coat of arms is what appears to be a single line. On close inspection, with the aid of a powerful magnifying glass, it is possible to read the hidden words

'Strength, Dignity and Laughter'. These were the words used by the Archbishop of Canterbury, Dr George Carey, to describe The Queen Mother during his sermon at her funeral service in Westminster Abbey on 9 April. 'Strength, dignity, laughter—three special qualities, earthed in her Christian life', said the Archbishop.

Asked for his reaction to his words being used on the miniature sheets, Dr Carey replied: 'The Crown Agents Stamp Bureau asked my permission and I am delighted the words have been included. It is a wonderful record of a truly remarkable lady.'

The process of reducing words to microsize is usually a security device and exemplifies the excellent technology now available to security printers to protect against fraud. Nigel Fordham, Head of the Crown Agents Stamp Bureau told *GSM*: 'To the best of my knowledge this is the

Miniature sheets contain portraits of The Queen Mother and scenes from her life. The designer particularly likes the Bermuda sheet (far left) because of its atmospheric honeymoon photograph

first time that this technique has been used with postage stamps.'

He added: 'These stamps are a vivid photographic record reflecting memorable moments in The Queen Mother's long life, which she lived to the full. She spanned the twentieth century, from the hansom cab to man walking on the moon. They also depict her unswerving and unselfish commitment to public duty.'

A tribute

In addition, a special Queen Mother philatelic souvenir sheet—'A Tribute From the Crown Agents Stamp Bureau' has also been produced for inclusion with this issue of *GSM*. This sheet, also printed on Crown Agents security watermarked paper, shows The Queen Mother, with her two daughters, The Queen and Princess Margaret, on the balcony of Buckingham Palace acknowledging the crowds on her 90th birthday.

Andrew Robinson designed the stamps and miniature sheets. In a short interview with *GSM* he explained that his brief from the Crown Agents Stamp Bureau was: 'To include two stamps, one to depict her in her youth or as the young Queen, whilst the other was to be a colour shot of her as The Queen Mother. The vignette images in the miniature sheets were to show her with members of the public, on official visits or with members of the Royal family. The issue was to have more of a celebratory feel than a sombre design.'

Asked how he interpreted the brief, he paused for a moment. 'The main inspiration was to make this stamp issue a celebration of The Queen Mother's life. The

designs were to be 'up beat' in an attempt to capture The Queen Mother's character. I believed that by showing her with members of the public ideally depicted this, especially during the war years. These shots really demonstrated her ability to relate to people and I wanted to show as many instances as I could find. I chose a neutral patterned background which was not too intrusive.'

Designs submitted by e-mail

'Did you submit several concepts for the souvenir sheetlets and stamps and if so please give details of the designs?' He replied: 'Other designs submitted to the Crown Agents Stamp Bureau showed similar images on different coloured backgrounds. Blues and purples were tried with variations on text style. The vignette principle remained pretty constant throughout the design stages. All of this was conducted through e-mail and no copies were kept.'

'How did you go about the picture research?' Andrew Robinson responded: 'Images were obtained through several

agencies including Rex, Alpha and Tim Graham. Hours were spent trawling through Hulton Getty's website. Corbis also had a site from which I chose an image. Most of the black and white images I used were from a Press Association CD. The remainder being taken from some prints sent to me by J S Library International.'

Asked why he selected yellow as the predominant colour of the miniature sheets, he explained that: 'Cream was the predominant colour on the background. The texture was a marbled effect created by using special software.'

Atmospheric

Finally, if he could only take one of the miniature sheets with him to show, as an example of his work, which would it be and why? 'I particularly like the Bermuda sheet because of the honeymoon shot with the wicker chairs. The photograph is very atmospheric and shows The Queen Mother and her husband the Duke of York, later to become King George VI, after a round of golf. The other photograph on this

A selection of the many portraits (and hats!) of The Queen Mother

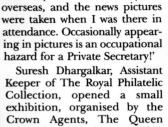

Elizabeth, I attended her on a wide variety of engagements over the years in this country and overseas, and the news pictures were taken when I was there in attendance. Occasionally appearing in pictures is an occupational hazard for a Private Secretary!'

Suresh Dhargalkar, Assistant Keeper of The Royal Philatelic Collection, opened a small exhibition, organised by the Crown Agents, The Queen Mother's Life in Stamps 1900–2002, at Osborne House, East Cowes, Isle of Wight, on Monday 5 August. Also on show were stamps issued to commemorate the 100th anniversary of the death of Queen Victoria and a display celebrating the arrival of the Benedictine monks on the Isle of Wight in 1901. Wightlink Isle of Wight Ferries sponsored the week-long exhibition, held in the Portuguese Room.

miniature sheet depicts The Queen Mother with her grandson, Prince Charles, and her long-serving Private Secretary, Captain Sir Alastair Aird, in the background.'

Sir Alastair Aird, Private Secretary to The Queen Mother, told *GSM*: 'Queen Elizabeth greatly enjoyed meeting people on her many engagements, and the pictures on the Crown Agents Stamp Bureau omnibus certainly bring back happy memories to me. I hope that these stamps will also give happy memories to the many people who either met Queen Elizabeth or saw her during her long life of public service.'

Sir Alastair Aird is depicted with The Queen Mother on the miniature sheets from Bermuda and Cayman Islands. Asked for his reaction, he replied: 'As for appearing on the stamps myself, that is simply coincidence. As Private Secretary to Queen

A Prince's Life

The life of Prince Charles as told on stamps, an overview by Paul Brittain

Sunday, 14 November 1948, and the crowds gathered outside Buckingham Palace to hear the news that Princess Elizabeth had given birth to a son: on 15 December he was christened Charles Philip Arthur George. Destined to remain the object of public interest and scrutiny, Charles' life has been largely played out for all to witness. It has not been easy, which may explain why few occasions in his life have been celebrated by stamps in their own right. Had circumstances been different, it seems certain that few Commonwealth stamp-issuing countries could have resisted his 50th birthday in 1998. Nevertheless, a substantial number of stamps have depicted Prince Charles at various times during his life, albeit these have mostly been as part of omnibus series celebrating Royal occasions associated with other members of the Royal Family.

Prince Charles at his christening (Antigua 1151)

In fact, Charles appears on a stamp when just one month old. To mark the Ruby Wedding Anniversary of The Queen in 1987, the $2 of the set from Antigua and the $6 miniature sheet from St Vincent showed Princess Elizabeth with Charles at his christening. His early years have been featured on several stamps, but the honour falls on New Zealand to have issued the first postage stamp to show Charles. In 1950 the annual Health pair depicted him in the arms of his mother. Two years later, a New Zealand Health stamp (2d. plus 1d.) again showed Charles, now as a toddler, the second stamp of the set showing Princess Anne as a baby. Many will also recall that the young Charles and Anne featured on National Savings stamps for some years.

Other stamps which show Charles in his early years include a number issued in 2002 to mark the Golden Jubilee of the Accession: they are Anguilla (30c.), Belize (75c.), St Helena (30p) and Tonga ($1.20), these showing Charles with Princess Elizabeth and Princess Anne. Charles is also shown with Anne, in 1951, on the 20v. value from Vanuatu to mark the Ruby Wedding Anniversary in 1987, while the $3 miniature sheet from Tuvalu for the same anniversary shows Charles at his sister's christening.

The Coronation

We all know how life changed for Princess Elizabeth in 1952: her Coronation took place on 2 June 1953. The events of the day were relived in 1977 with the Silver Jubilee omnibus series from the Crown Agents. After the ceremony, all gathered at Buckingham Palace, the family group seen on the 25p value from Tristan da Cunha. A similar view was shown on the £2 issued by British Indian Ocean Territory to mark the 50th anniversary of the Coronation in 2003.

However, what the crowds were waiting for, then as on many occasions, was the appearance on the balcony. This featured on the 55c. Silver Jubilee from Turks and Caicos Islands (part of the Crown Agents' omnibus), and also on the $1 Silver Jubilee from Aitutaki (Cook Islands).

The famous gathering on the balcony of Buckingham Palace has been featured on several stamps since, some in 2003. These include the 80c. (plus 70c. as a miniature sheet) from Bahamas, 45p (plus 95p as a miniature sheet) from British Antarctic Territory, $5 from British Virgin Islands, and from the Cook Islands. The 35p from Ascension in 1999, part of the set to mark the Queen Mother's Century, is another to capture the scene from 1953.

The Coronation might have been the occasion when a stamp first appeared from the British Post Office depicting Prince Charles. Among the many design ideas submitted was one from the stamp printers, Harrison and Sons, featuring a 'family group'; however, this was rejected by the advisory panel.

The family gathered on the balcony of Buckingham Palace on other occasions has also been recorded on stamps, such as following the Trooping of the Colour, depicted by Grenada in 1991 to mark the 65th

Queen's Coronation: Tristan da Cunha 214

Coronation balcony scenes: Aitutaki 228; Bahamas 1316

With Queen Mother: Ascension 782

Trooping of the Colour: Tanzania 517

The young Prince: New Zealand 701/2 and 711

The Queen, Anne and Charles: St Helena 849; Vanuatu 487

GRENADINES OF ST. VINCENT

$2   1986 ROYAL WEDDING

At Prince Andrew's wedding: Grenadines of St Vincent 484

Swaziland 70c

The Prince with parents and sister: Swaziland 712

Early years: Penrhyn Island 223/5

Royal Wedding: Aitutaki 412

$1   27TH BIRTHDAY 1 JULY 1982 H.R.H. THE PRINCESS OF WALES

AITUTAKI COOK ISLANDS

Investiture: Great Britain 806

19

Castell Y Waun / Chirk Castle, Clwyd, Cymru / Wales

25th anniversary of Investiture: Great Britain 1810

It was his sense of duty to the nation that persuaded Charles to leave the Navy in 1976

birthday of The Queen (15c.) and by Tanzania in 1987 on the 60th birthday (5s.).

In 1986, on the occasion of the wedding of Prince Andrew, a $1 stamp from the Grenadines of St Vincent featured a balcony scene with Charles, Prince Andrew, Princess Anne and Princess Margaret.

Education

The first school Charles attended was Hill House in Kensington, West London, followed by Cheam School in Berkshire. It was then to Scotland and Gordonstoun, a period which he did not find totally fulfilling. Charles nevertheless enjoyed a short break from Gordonstoun, spending some time at Timbertops, an outstation of Geelong Grammar School in Australia. The Press mainly respected the family's wishes, so photographs were only permitted on pre-arranged occasions.

Charles as a young boy is seen on the 70s. value from Swaziland to mark The Queen's Golden Jubilee in 2002, while the set issued by Penrhyn (Cook Islands) in 1981 to mark his wedding features Charles at various stages of his education. A similar 'potted history' was provided by Antigua (also existing with Barbuda overprint) on stamps issued in booklet form for the wedding.

An idea of how Charles' life is determined for him is evident by the fact that The Queen held a dinner to discuss his further education on leaving school. It is reported that while The Queen listened, she did not participate in the discussions. The outcome was that Charles attended Trinity College at Cambridge, before embarking on a career with the Royal Navy, attending the Royal Naval College at Dartmouth, although prior to that he did spend a short time with the Royal Air Force at Cranwell. It was his sense of duty to the nation that persuaded Charles to leave the Navy in 1976.

Prince of Wales

While at Cheam School, Charles was allowed to listen to the closing ceremony of the 1958 British Empire and Commonwealth Games in Cardiff. Although unable to be personally present, The Queen used the occasion to announce that she was creating Prince Charles as Prince of Wales. For a 10 year old schoolboy, he already had a formidable list of titles: Earl of Chester, Duke of Cornwall, Duke of Rothesay, Earl of Carrick, Lord of the Isles and Baron of Renfrew, and Prince and Great Steward of Scotland.

His Investiture as Prince of Wales took place in 1969, providing the first occasion when Prince Charles appeared on a British postage stamp. Work started on the stamps two years in advance, it being suggested that the designs should either be based on

a portrait of the Prince, or feature buildings and scenes of Wales, or be symbolic of Wales. Five artists were invited to submit ideas, Roy Morgan and David Jones from Wales, and three who had previously designed British stamps, Rosalind Dease, David Gentleman and Jeffery Matthews. As is known, Gentleman's ideas were accepted, the issued stamps featuring the King's Gate, the Eagle Tower and the Queen's Gate of Caernarvon Castle, where the Investiture ceremony took place, a Celtic Cross from Margam Abbey, and a portrait of the Prince.

Gentleman submitted alternative ideas, likewise featuring Caernarvon Castle, including an aerial view, and the Celtic Cross, but with all designs including a profile portrait of the Prince.

The issued stamps had the portrait appearing on just the 1s. value, although again two approaches had been tried, one with a profile portrait, and the three-quarters portrait as used. The stamps were issued on the day of the Investiture, 1 July 1969: in those days errors were quite common on British stamps, so all values are known with the phosphor omitted, while the *se-tenant* strip of three 5d. can be found with either the black, red or deep grey omitted.

While first day covers were by this stage extremely popular, the idea of pictorial handstamps had not been introduced by the Post Office, and privately sponsored handstamps were few. Only three have designs linked with the Investiture stamps, from Margam Abbey, for Croeso 69 at Cardiff, and for the Talyllyn Railway.

Equally, the idea of an omnibus series for every conceivable Royal occasion was still undeveloped. It was not until 1981 that an overseas country featured the Investiture on a stamp, that being Antigua on one of the stamps in booklet form (already mentioned) issued on the occasion of his wedding.

Royal Mail also celebrated the 25th anniversary of the Investiture on St David's Day (1 March) 1994 with five stamps that reproduce paintings by the Prince, two of Wales, and one each of England, Scotland

Gilbert Islands 48

SILVER JUBILEE 8c

Gilbert Islands

SILVER JUBILEE QUEEN ELIZABETH
H.R.H. PRINCE OF WALES' VISIT 1973

CAYMAN ISLANDS

and Northern Ireland. The situation as regards special handstamps had now completely changed, so not only did Royal Mail provide two pictorial 'first day of issue' handstamps, but there were 20 which were sponsored on the day appropriate to this issue.

Wedding

22 July 1981 was the day of the wedding of Prince Charles to Lady Diana Spencer. The occasion naturally provides a wealth of stamp portraits, for this was when 'Royal stamp fever' really took off. The following year saw the 21st birthday of Lady Diana, the philatelic celebrations including an omnibus series from the Crown Agents. One stamp from each set showed part of the wedding ceremony from 1981. Aitutaki (Cook Islands) also used its 21st birthday set to look back to the wedding ($1 value).

In 2003 St Vincent issued a set to mark the fifth anniversary of the death of Diana, the $2 value of which recalled the wedding.

This phase in the Prince's life was well covered by Niue at the time, with appropriate sets, not only for the wedding and for the 21st birthday of the Princess of Wales, but also for the birth of Prince William in 1982, the theme being continued through to the Christmas stamps of that year.

In 1991 several of the countries whose stamps were handled at the time by the Inter-Governmental Philatelic Corporation issued sets to mark the 10th anniversary of the wedding. It was in the following year that the rift in the marriage became obvious to the media and public.

Public life

Visits are on the agenda of all members of the Royal Family, not least Charles, although relevant stamps are not numerous. The Silver Jubilee omnibus from the Crown Agents in 1977 provided the opportunity to recall two earlier visits, one in 1970 to the Gilbert Islands (8c. value) and in 1973 to the West Indies, which included the Cayman Islands (8c.). That latter visit was also remembered by Anguilla on the 25c. value of its Silver Jubilee set, the stamps and miniature sheets being re-issued later in the year overprinted 'ROYAL VISIT TO WEST INDIES'.

In 1989 the Prince visited Hong Kong, the event being commemorated at the time by a set of four stamps, while ten years later, in 1999, a visit to the Falkland Islands was marked by a £2 stamp. On the

occasion of the 50th anniversary of the end of the Second World War and the liberation of the Channel Islands in 1995, the Prince visited Guernsey and Jersey, the visit being celebrated by Guernsey with a £1.50 stamp issued on the day of the visit, 9 May.

If one were building a thematic collection around the life of Prince Charles, then his undisguised admiration of the radio comedy series 'The Goons' could well be recalled by the Great Britain 17p stamp from 1985 for British Film Year featuring Peter Sellers.

The Prince is also well known for his love of polo and skiing. It seems that the 65th birthday of The Queen in 1991 was seen as the perfect opportunity to show the Prince playing polo, for such scenes appeared on the 25c. from the Grenadines of Grenada, the 10l. from Sierra Leone and the 70s. from Uganda.

Charles skiing with Prince William is shown on the £1 stamp issued by British Indian Ocean Territory in 2003 on the occasion of his elder son's 21st birthday.

Family life

Prince Charles has two sons, William and Harry. The line of succession means that Prince William is often in the limelight, resulting in stamp issues for both his 18th and 21st birthdays, in 2000 and 2003. Several of the stamps show William with his father. One particularly pleasing set was issued by Kiribati in 2000, the four values—25c., 60c., 75c. and $1—tracing the life of William.

With Prince William:
Kiribati 615/8

Peter Sellers:
Great Britain 1298

Polo: Uganda 960

Skiing: British Indian Ocean Islands 287

William's birth in 1982 was marked by Niue, including the Christmas stamps of that year, with the 80c. plus 5c. value showing him as a baby in his parents' arms.

Harry's birth in 1984 was commemorated by Aitutaki (Cook Islands), the $2.10 stamp including Diana and William.

Both William and Harry when young are shown with their father on the 45p stamp issued by Tristan da Cunha on William's 18th birthday. On the same occasion Gibraltar issued a 54p stamp showing Charles with William.

Cayman Islands 427   Hong Kong 626

Anguilla 298

Falkland Islands 837

Royal visits

Guernsey 680

With Princes William and Henry: Tristan da Cunha 683

With Prince William: Gibraltar 934

Celebrating The Queen Mother's 100th birtday: Great Britain MS2161

At Garter ceremony with The Queen Mother: Ghana MS1143

Family gathering marking The Queen Mother's 80th birthday: Bermuda 495

Prince Charles driving car: Fiji 1062

Of all the members of the Royal Family, the one who has enjoyed the most sustained admiration of the British public has been The Queen Mother. Sadly to miss her daughter's Golden Jubilee celebrations, nevertheless to live 100 years is no mean achievement. The affection felt has been expressed by several stamp issues, most notable since her 80th birthday, often recalling events from her life, naturally often including Prince Charles.

A number have shown Charles with The Queen Mother at the Garter Ceremony, several as part of 'The Life and Times of Her Majesty Queen Elizabeth The Queen Mother' omnibus series instigated by the Crown Agents in 1985. These include the 25c. issued by Fiji, plus the 110c. miniature sheet from Ghana, and the $2 miniature sheet from the Turks and Caicos Islands.

Birthdays have provided opportunities for family gatherings, the 30c. from Bermuda for the 'Life and Times' omnibus showing The Queen Mother on her 80th birthday with her grandchildren. The $1 miniature sheet also recalls the same birthday celebration.

In 1999 the Crown Agents marked The Queen Mother's Century, the $3 stamp from Fiji showing The Queen Mother with Charles in 1986. The family gathered featured on the $1.50 stamp from the British Virgin Islands in 2000 to mark The Queen Mother's 100th year.

That 100th birthday was also celebrated by Royal Mail with a miniature sheet and prestige stamp booklet. The photograph of the family gathering seen on the sheet was specially commissioned by Royal Mail. Among the special handstamps available for the day of issue (4 August 2000) was one showing the exterior of Clarence House, and another featuring a map to show its location. At the time the home of The Queen Mother, the Prince's links with Clarence House are on-going, and it was in fact his home from July 1949 when his parents moved from Buckingham Palace.

(Clarence House has featured on other handstamps when stamps have been issued by Royal Mail to honour The Queen Mother.)

A new phase

So now Prince Charles embarks on a new phase of his life following his marriage to Camilla Parker-Bowles, with two new informal photographs for the stamp album from Royal Mail. For Camilla this is of course a philatelic first. Hopefully it is not too churlish to mention that her great-grandmother, Alice Keppel, has appeared on a British stamp, one of the Greetings stamps of 1995 with their theme of 'Greetings in Art'.

To end our review, first a bit part. In 1993, as part of a set marking Anniversaries and Events, Sierra Leone issued a 100l. to mark the 40th anniversary of the Coronation. Although the stamp shows The Queen with Princess Anne, do one of the pair of legs seen behind belong to Prince Charles? And for the best philatelic portrait of Charles, one probably turns the pages to Jersey, and the Royal Silver Wedding of 1972, with a fine portrait on the 7½ p stamp.

Alice Keppel: Great Britain 1864

Best portrait: Jersey 83

Prince William Stamps are Front Page News

The Crown Agents Stamp Bureau issues for Prince William's 18th birthday received extraordinary publicity in the national press. Peter Jennings FRPSL explains how this PR coup was achieved

I had intended to write a story about the four attractive stamps to be issued by Jersey Post. However, before I could, the story broke in the John McEntee column in *The Express* on 11 April, 'Putting stamp on Will's pin-up image'.

The story began: 'Prince William's aversion to the camera had caused a major headache for the designer of a special edition of stamps marking the heir to the throne's 18th birthday. Because of the paucity of photocalls, designer William Wall had relatively little to work on for four digitally-manipulated portraits of the Prince to be released by Jersey Post for his birthday on June 21.'

A sheet from the Crown Agents omnibus issue and the Gibraltar stamp depicting Diana, Princess of Wales

It was not long before other national newspapers picked up the story. PA News ran the story with pictures on 14 April under the catchy headline: 'Birthday Boy William Stars on Stamps'.

Two days later, on 16 April, PA put out a follow-up story: 'Castle Error On Prince William Birthday Stamps.' The background to one of the stamps was supposed to have included Prince William's face with the backdrop of Caernarfon Castle in North Wales, where Prince Charles's investiture as Prince of Wales took place. In fact, the stamp depicted nearby Beaumaris Castle.

So, more stories about stamps in the national press. No publicity is bad publicity —if given a positive spin!

On 18 April PA News put out a story of mine under the headline 'Pleas to Royal Mail over Prince's Birthday'. The story, written by Peter Archer, PA's distinguished Court Correspondent, began: 'Prince William's 18th birthday will be celebrated on postage stamps around the world—but so far Royal Mail has no commemorative issue planned for mainland Britain.

'As well as a stamp for sale in Jersey, birthday stamps will be issued in the Isle of Man, Ascension Island, British Virgin Islands, Cayman Islands, Falkland Islands, Fiji, South Georgia and South Sandwich Islands, and Tristan da Cunha.

'The Isle of Man Post Office is also releasing a commemorative souvenir sheet based on the format adopted by the Crown Agents Omnibus.'

The story continued: 'Top philatelist Peter Jennings called on Royal Mail to follow suit and issue a special stamp to commemorate William's 18th Birthday on 21 June', with a suggestion from me that 'Royal Mail should issue a single first-class stamp depicting an informal picture of Prince William.'

In May Royal Mail and Buckingham Palace asked the Press Association to put out the story about the Royal Mail miniature sheet of four 27p stamps to be issued on 4 August to celebrate the 100th Birthday of Her Majesty Queen Elizabeth The Queen Mother.

The story, written by Peter Archer, and a picture of the sheetlet depicting The Queen, The Queen Mother, Prince Charles and a very formal looking Prince William, was strictly embargoed until 14 May.

At Earls Court on 22 May, late on the first day of The Stamp Show 2000, I interviewed Mark Thomson, Managing Director of Royal Mail Stamps & Collectibles, on behalf of *GSM*.

I pursued the idea of a special single 27p 1st class Royal Mail stamp to mark Prince William's 18th Birthday. He responded with an emphatic 'No' when asked if Royal Mail planned such an issue. A pity. At the time Royal Mail was planning a special stamp label depicting the England football team and four greetings stamps to be issued, had England won Euro 2000!

The timing of a story is absolutely vital to its likely success. On 7 June, Nigel Fordham, Head of The Crown Agents Stamp Bureau, and I, met Martin Keene, former PA Royal photographer and now Picture Editor, at PA News, to discuss my story about the Prince William omnibus.

We selected two sheetlets of five stamps —Tristan da Cunha and South Georgia & South Sandwich Islands, from 'The Life and Times of Prince William' produced by The Crown Agents Stamp Bureau on behalf of seven countries to celebrate Prince William's 18th birthday.

The Crown Agents co-ordinated the concept and production of the sheetlets and 28 single stamps, which were sanctioned by St James's Palace, and approved by Her Majesty The Queen.

My story mentioned that designer Andrew Robinson used images of Prince William taken over the past 18 years of his life by the distinguished royal photographer Tim Graham.

'Sunday for Monday' is always a good time to release stories about stamps and mid-morning on Sunday 11 June PA News released my article, together with pictures of the two sheetlets.

The PA news desk telephoned me early on Saturday evening and asked if any of the stamps featured Princess Diana,

Unaccepted designs by Derek Miller, photographs of Caernarfon Castle, courtesy of Vic Guy

Unaccepted designs by Andrew Robinson (above) and Crown Agents Stamp Bureau Studios (below)

mother of Prince William. The answer was no, but after 30 years in journalism, I knew this particular stamp story was likely to attract massive media coverage. It did!

PA added colour to the story: 'A series of 35 stamps chronicle Prince William's life from his first salute with a cheeky grin to a formal royal wave. They show the young Prince at play and at work, from him running alongside his first pony to making his way to school.'

The story continued: 'One stamp features the young prince's father, but none feature his mother, Diana, Princess of Wales. Some capture the shyness of his early teenage years, as he glances away from the camera lens, but later images show a confident Prince, who has come into his own as he waves to his millions of fans.'

'Each set is presented in a sheet with a backdrop of William beside the loch at Balmoral. The stamps variously depict him on his own or with his brother Prince Harry, and in one case with the Prince of Wales.'

The story included quotes from Nigel Fordham and myself which were widely used in the national and international press.

My telephone rang continuously during Sunday. One of the callers was Eileen, the wife of photographer, Tim Graham, who told me that *The Times* Picture Desk wanted to use a photograph of one of the Tristan da Cunha stamps on the front page.

The following day, Monday, 12 June, the story, together with pictures of the two sheetlets, was used in *The Times*, the *Daily Telegraph, Daily Mail, The Express, The Mirror, The Sun,* the *Daily Record, The Scotsman,* and *The Birmingham Post,* to name but a selection.

The Times used a wonderful picture by Tim Graham on the front page. Yes, a large colour picture, together with the names of the seven countries included in the caption. Two more pictures of stamps were used in black and white with the story 'Stamps mark coming of age' by Dominic Kennedy.

The Sun headline ran 'Birthday boy Wills stamps his authority'. The *Daily Telegraph* chose 'Stamps fit for a future king'. The *Daily Star* went for 'Birthday boy Wills has 'em licked ...'

Several of the papers highlighted the fact that Princess Diana was not included on any of the stamps. Headlines included: 'Diana left off 18th birthday stamps', *The Mirror*, and 'How stamp chiefs removed Diana from the Prince's life', *The Express*.

Derek Miller, the well-known stamp designer, submitted speculative designs to the Crown Agents Stamp Bureau. He revealed to me that his brief from the Crown Agents specifically mentioned that Princess Diana was not to be included on any of the stamps.

None of Derek Miller's design concepts were selected, but I am sure that *GSM* readers will enjoy studying them, as well as other unissued designs by Andrew Robinson, and CASB Studios. These are reproduced by courtesy of the Crown Agents Stamp Bureau.

Concerned about the Princess Diana controversy, Nigel Fordham and I discussed the matter and I gave another story to PA News.

This concerned the 30p stamp issued by Gibraltar to mark Prince William's birthday, which did show Princess Diana.

The story quoted Nigel Fordham: 'The 30p value stamp bears a portrait of Princess Diana holding Prince William taken at Kensington Palace, as well as a decorative label within the stamp sheet which includes a picture of the Princess with other members of The Royal Family.'

The papers loved it. 'A stamp for Mummy' was the headline in the *Daily Mail* which included a colour picture of the stamp and the caption: 'In his mother's arms: Baby William is shown with Diana on new stamp.'

The Mirror also included a colour picture of the Gibraltar stamp with the headline 'Rock's Stamp For Di' together with a story by Jane Kerr, Royal Reporter. The *Daily Record* headline ran: 'Stamps Snub Di Back In The Picture'.

The *Mail* then ran a further two pages 'What those stamps don't begin to reveal' together with illustrations of several of the stamps in colour. Two days later, on 15 June, the *Mail* devoted a further two pages 'Untold stories behind those Royal stamps ...'.

The next day, 16 June, *The Times* included colour illustrations of seven of the stamps to illustrate a story 'Zooming in on Wills' published in *Times 2 Media*. That morning BBC Breakfast showed the pre-recorded television interview with Nigel Fordham, commenting about the Crown Agents' Prince William omnibus.

Without doubt, this particular PR effort resulted in massive regional, national and international media attention and, once again, significantly raised the profile of the 'Hobby of Kings and King of Hobbies'.

Readers will note that one of the design concepts commissioned by the Crown Agents comprised sheetlets of nine stamps; I feel this would have been excessive. We may certainly expect to see Prince William Engagement stamps, Wedding stamps, and Coronation stamps as well as stamps marking his visits to all parts of the world. Therefore, it's vital that the Crown Agents Stamp Bureau sets an example and doesn't kill the goose that lays the golden eggs!

Elizabeth, The Queen Mother on Stamps

Following recent issues celebrating The Queen Mother's 100th year, Bernard Towler reviews her earlier appearances on stamps

This stamp story of the Queen Mother is being put together shortly after the celebration of her 99th birthday. The way in which that day was marked encourages us to look forward to 4 August 2000, the day of her birth centenary.

Although born into a noble Scottish family, her birth took place at St Paul's Walden Bury, in Hertfordshire. In 1904 her father became the 14th Earl of Strathmore and much of her childhood was spent in their Scottish home, Glamis Castle. During World War I, part of the castle became a hospital for wounded servicemen and the young Lady Elizabeth Bowes-Lyon helped nurse them.

The war was over before Elizabeth met her future husband, Prince Albert, second son of King George V and Queen Mary. They married in 1923, by which time he was Duke of York. In 1927 the Duke and Duchess went to Australasia for a long tour. Unlike later royal tours, their visit was not recorded on stamps. Her first appearance, and her only one as Duchess of York, did not come until 1932. And it's not surprising that the first place in the Empire to picture her on stamps was Newfoundland.

The first Queen Mother stamp

This former colony did not join the Dominion of Canada until 1949, being the last of Canada's provinces to do so, a decision only then taken because of Newfoundland's poor financial situation. During its long period of independence, a large number of attractive stamps were issued. Many pictured members of the royal family, some not seen elsewhere—a 1911 set including The Duke of Connaught (Queen Victoria's third son) and Prince John, youngest son of King George V and

Queen Mary, who died in his early teens. Then, in January 1932, Newfoundland issued the first stamp to show the young Princess Elizabeth, followed (in August) by one showing her mother (SG 226). That first Queen Mother stamp is not scarce, apart from the three listed varieties. The first has a 14 line perforation instead of the normal comb perf 13½. The others are imperf between and imperforate pairs, only listed in mint condition.

There were no more philatelic appearances of Elizabeth while she was Duchess of York. Her father-in-law, King George V, died in January 1936 and Edward, Prince of Wales, became King. Before the year was out, however, he had abdicated and Elizabeth's beloved Bertie took his place. His coronation, indeed their coronation, was fixed for 12 May 1937. With time to make the necessary preparations and the experience gained by that first major British Empire 'omnibus' stamp series for the late King's silver jubilee, Elizabeth and her husband were seen on stamps in every continent.

Coronation robes

Though a stamp collector 'on and off' for 58 years, I have only just woken up to the fact that all those coronation stamps were not released on the same day, the day of the coronation. Indeed, some of those many pink patches on the world's map did not have coronation stamps at all. You could say that of Australia, but it could also

be held that the new definitives, which began to appear there from May 1937, formed, when complete, a 'coronation definitive' set. The first two values appeared on 10 May, two days before the coronation, with the 2d. showing the new King and the 1d. (165) picturing Queen Elizabeth—her first appearance since 1932 in Newfoundland. Some of the later values in that set showed neither King nor Queen but various Australian animals and birds. However, not only did further values picture the King but the 5s. (176) showed a full-length view of Queen Elizabeth, in coronation robes, while the 10s. similarly pictured the King. Later still came the £1 stamp (178), showing them together, complete with their crowns.

The Dominion of Canada, still of course minus Newfoundland, had a single coronation stamp (356) showing the royal couple. This also appeared two days before their day of crowning.

Then, on the day itself, came the omnibus set for all except those territories which either 'did it their own way' or, as we will see, omitted to have a coronation issue at all. This series showed the King and Queen, in the same design for all three values, though colours differed. Printing was shared between De La Rue and Bradbury Wilkinson.

Never in India

Generally, every territory which had a set of four George V jubilee stamps in that omnibus series, also had its three for the coronation. Exceptions were Aden, which had no jubilee set but had one for the coronation, and India—which had a set of seven values (not in the omnibus design) for the jubilee, but nothing at all for the coronation. Indeed, the Queen Mother has never appeared on an Indian stamp. Newfoundland, which had a straight set of four stamps in the jubilee series, did the same for the coronation, so Elizabeth appeared there again in 1937. Her husband was also shown on a long set of 11 coronation pictorials, special to that very loyal colony. For South Africa (and also South West Africa, now Namibia), coronation sets showed only the King.

Northern Rhodesia had a normal omnibus set, but Southern Rhodesia provided another exception, with its four values (36/9), showing the King and Queen against a background of the Victoria Falls. These stamps also appeared on 12 May.

The one British coronation stamp, a 1½d. value (461) showing the King and Queen, appeared the day after the coronation. Was

Elizabeth's first appearance on stamps, as Duchess of York (Newfoundland 226), and as Queen (Australia 165) Coronation issues from Malta, Southern Rhodesia and GB

In coronation robes on Australia 176

that because postal staff were on holiday for coronation day? That stamp was also issued with overprints and surcharges in Spanish or French currency for British post offices in Morocco and also overprinted (but not surcharged) for use in the International zone of Tangier.

Also on 13 May, came New Zealand's distinctive set of three coronation stamps, showing the new King and Queen. Those stamps were overprinted for the New Zealand dependency of Niue and also for the Cook Islands, the latter producing a variety of a small final 'S' for the abbreviated 'IS'DS'.

Before and after World War II, there were several royal visits and they produced some stamps showing the Queen Mother. She is there with King George on a stamp (374) in Canada's 1939 royal visit set.

Family group

Then, in 1947, there was a visit to Southern Africa. The two princesses went with the King and Queen and some of that visit's issues reflect this. Identical designs were used for Basutoland (now Lesotho) and Bechuanaland (now Botswana) and Swaziland. In each set the royal couple appear together on one of the four values and in a family group on another. The 1947 South African set has the King and Queen together on one of three stamps (112) This set was also overprinted for use in South West Africa.

There was also a pair of stamps (62/3) for Southern Rhodesia (now Zimbabwe), with the ½d. value showing the princesses and the 1d. their parents. Only three weeks after those stamps, a set of four was issued, each one showing one of those royal visitors, the 1d. (64) showing Queen Elizabeth. These are described as Southern Rhodesia's Victory issue.

During her years as Queen Consort, she was pictured alone on only a few other stamps. Newfoundland, scene of her philatelic debut as Duchess of York, showed her as Queen Elizabeth on the 3c. (269) in a set of four royal portraits, which do not appear to have commemorated any specific event. That portrait of her is similar to the earlier one, with the addition of a coronet.

Australia continued showing the Queen on some definitives, with the King on others. She is seen on the 1942 1d. and 1½d. values (203/4) in designs which differ only in their frames. The 1½d. was reissued

The 1947 royal visit to southern Africa— issues from Bechuanaland (133), Swaziland (45), South Africa (112) and Southern Rhodesia (63)

in 1949 without watermark. Then, during 1950/51, they were replaced by new low values, a more close-up portrait of the Queen on the 1½d. and 2d. (236/7)

The 25th anniversary of the wedding of Queen Elizabeth and King George occurred on 26 April 1948. And on that day two British stamps commemorating this event were issued (493/4). They were also overprinted for use in the British Post Offices in the Persian Gulf, Morocco and Tangier. Their denominations, 2½d. and £1, set a pattern of one low and one high value, which was followed in the omnibus set issued later for a wide range of colonies and protectorates—this being the first British royal anniversary to be marked by issues for the various Malayan states. There were no special issues for Australia, Canada or New Zealand, nor for Southern Rhodesia, as it then was. A single 3d. value was issued in South Africa, in bilingual pairs (125) and this stamp was also overprinted for use in South West Africa. All of these Silver Wedding stamps show the King and Queen together.

After the death of King George VI in 1952 and the accession of Queen Elizabeth II, the Queen Mother (as she then became) was not seen on stamps for a long while. In 1975 a single 20p stamp (123), issued in

Southern Rhodesia's Victory issue (64)

Newfoundland 269

Australia 204 and 237

1948 Silver Wedding issues from Great Britain (493/4) and South Africa bi-lingual pair (125)

80th birthday—Great Britain 1129 and St Helena 366

44

Jersey to mark her visit there, showed a Cecil Beaton photograph. This was a fore-runner of many informal pictures of her, to be seen on the vast numbers of stamps which have been issued to celebrate the Queen Mother's birthdays.

That flow began in 1980, with 41 stamps plus 12 miniature sheets from 29 countries, marking Her Majesty's 80th birthday. All those earlier pictures were contemporary and also rather formal, often showing her wearing a tiara. Three examples of the wide variety of this 80th birthday output are the lone British 12p stamp (1129), showing a close-up, complete with a vivid blue feathered hat. Anguilla's set of four, plus a miniature sheet (411/5) is equally close, but the hat is very different. However, St Helena's 24p stamp (366) is among those offering a somewhat more formal yet very happy picture, still with a tiara.

226 stamps from 50 countries!

In 1985 the number of countries marking the Queen Mother's 85th birthday rose to 50, while the output jumped to 226 stamps and 47 miniature sheets. And those are only the ones which made it to full catalogue listing. Some Queen Mother stamps have been consigned to the catalogue's appendices. Tuvalu went over the top for that same birthday. Formerly the Ellice Islands, only one stamp appeared for the 80th birthday, increasing to eight in 1985, plus a miniature sheet (334/42). However, additional 'Leaders of the World' sets issued for each of eight separate islands were demoted to the appendix.

Maybe chastened by this, Tuvalu gave the Queen Mother's 90th and 95th birthdays a miss! Antigua's apparently uninhabited island of Redonda also had two stamps for the 1980 birthday and three for the 85th, all of which received similar catalogue treatment.

Those 1985 issues, titled 'The Life and Times of Queen Elizabeth the Queen Mother', varied greatly in content, with plenty of variety in the headgear. This ranged from the coronation crown on the Seychelles/Zil Elwannyen Sesel 1 rupee (115), through many different hats to none at all on the Swaziland 15c. (487). They also were true to their collective title, in taking us back to the Queen Mother's early life—and much further back than that 1937 coronation. Antigua-Barbuda's set of

seven (776/82) moves from a photograph taken when she was seven on the 15c., to a picture of the Queen Mother receiving flowers from children, on her 82nd birthday on the $3.

There was no British set for the 85th birthday, but a set of four charming pictures of the Queen Mother came in 1990 (1507/10). Again, like those Barbuda stamps, they spanned her life, though this time they moved from a contemporary portrait on the lowest 20p value, on to one as Queen (taken by Dorothy Wilding) and another as Duchess of York, to that same childhood photo (stated to have been taken by Rita Martin) on the 37p stamp.

The 90th birthday inspired a British Commonwealth total of 127 stamps, plus 22 miniature sheets. This reversal of the earlier trend continued in 1995, when the figures were down to 55 and 16. Do two related reasons explain this? It might be a reaction against too many stamps in 1985, or that the wide range of pictures shown then (many of them excellent) may have left few fresh ones which might encourage collectors to purchase the stamps. However, stamp users who do not collect are unlikely to have seen many stamps from abroad. So, if the picture is new to them, they may buy the stamps for their mail. But then, if stamps were only produced to serve their postal purpose, we would surely see far fewer produced. And that's not counting Redonda and other uninhabited isles.

A happy, relaxed picture

1990 saw the first Queen Mother commemorative from The Isle of Man (448), another smiling picture with yet another hat. I'm sure that Queen Mother stamps could provide a substantial start to a thematic collection of hats. However, tiaras were not forgotten in 1990. The 10c. (1045) from the Turks and Caicos set provides a very happy, relaxed picture, despite that formal headdress.

Many colonies used identical designs in 1995. They included what must be the most controversial Queen Mother picture so far seen on a stamp. This is a pastel drawing of the Queen Mother (St Vincent and The Grenadines, 2927, or Maldive Islands, 2274). These were printed in sheetlets with three other pictures, more in line with what had gone before. The Cook Islands/Aitutaki offering is one lovely stamp (688) which, for once, lacks a hat.

A well-chosen selection

So much for the many British Commonwealth stamps celebrating landmarks in our Queen Mother's life. What about the rest of the World? A fairly quick search through the foreign volumes of *Stamps of the World* revealed two sets from Liberia. The 1985 set, for her 85th birthday, has three values (1621/3). These show her in garter robes, at the races and waving to the crowds—surely a well-chosen selection of her activities? The second set of two was issued in 1991, marking the Queen Mother's 90th birthday. The 10c. illustrated there (1809), shows an almost full-length portrait of her as a girl. This matches one in a *Mail on Sunday* supplement for her 95th birthday, which (it was stated) was taken in 1906, when she was six-years-old. There was also a $2 value (1810), showing her as Duchess of York. One other foreign item, consigned, however, to the appendices, was a 1500f. value from Burkina Faso, issued for the 85th birthday.

None of these birthdays has been commemorated in Australia, although the Queen Mother does appear on this year's Queen's birthday stamp (1870). Brilliant red and blue colours show her with The Queen. Now we look forward to the philatelic celebration of Her Majesty The Queen Mother's centenary on 4 August 2000. Despite some excesses, back in 1985, there will surely be many special stamps issued around the world. Let's hope they are worthy of the occasion and of our Queen Mother.

1975 visit to Jersey (Jersey 123)

Australia 1870

85th birthday—Zil Elwannyen Sesel 115, Swaziland 487 and Barbuda 776

90th birthday—Great Britain 1508

95th birthday— Liberia 1809

HRH The Princess Margaret, Herself a Collector, Depicted on Stamps

Peter Jennings FRPSL recalls some of the many stamps to have shown Princess Margaret and asks whether Royal Mail would now consider issuing a stamp in her memory.

HRH The Princess Margaret, Countess of Snowdon 1930-2002, was a keen stamp collector. I am able to reveal this little known aspect of the late Princess from a letter which Viscount Ullswater, her Private Secretary, sent me in March 2000. It read, in part: 'Princess Margaret has asked me to write to thank you, and Mr Tim Graham (Royal photographer), for your kindness in sending her a copy of your book, *The Queen Mother's Century Celebrated in Stamps.*'

'The Princess, herself a keen collector of stamps, was fascinated to see the various issues which reflect the life and activities of Queen Elizabeth The Queen Mother, and Her Royal Highness is delighted to have this wonderful record to keep.'

Princess Margaret herself was depicted on a number of stamps from UK Overseas Territories, and Commonwealth countries issued by the Crown Agents. My personal selection includes a number of stamps showing Princess Margaret with her sister, HM The Queen, and other members of The Royal Family.

Princess Margaret, the younger daughter of the then Duke and Duchess of York, was born on 21 August 1930 in Scotland, at Glamis Castle in Angus, the ancestral home of her mother, the former Lady Elizabeth Bowes-Lyon, daughter of the Earl of Strathmore and Kinghorne.

First appearance

The young Princess Margaret first appeared on a 1c. stamp issued by Canada, on 15 May 1939, together with her elder sister, Princess Elizabeth, to commemorate the Royal Visit that year (SG 108).

A picture of the two princesses taken during 1939 is shown on a 20c. stamp issued by Jamaica as part of 'The Queen's 60th Birthday' omnibus, issued on 21 April 1986 (646).

Princess Margaret made her first solo appearance on a triangular 'New Zealand health stamp issued on 1 October 1943 (636). The following year Princesses Margaret and Elizabeth were depicted together on the two health stamps issued in 1944 (665/6).

The two princesses were also featured together, and in some cases with their parents also, on stamps issued to commemorate the Royal Visit to Southern Africa during 1947. These included South Africa (113), South West Africa (136), Basutoland (34/5); Bechuanaland (134/5) and Swaziland (44/5), all issued on 17 February.

Southern Rhodesia issued a ½d. stamp showing the two princesses (62) on 1 April, followed on 8 May by a 6d. 'Victory' stamp (67) featuring a delightful portrait of Princess Margaret.

The Royal Family is depicted on a 2d. New Zealand 'Peace' issue stamp (670)

issued on 1 April 1946. This stamp was overprinted for use in the Cook Islands (147), Niue (99) and Samoa (216), all issued on 4 June.

A St Helena £1.50 miniature sheet (MS794), issued locally on 3 September 1999 to celebrate 'The Queen Mother's Centenary', shows King George VI and Queen Elizabeth and their daughters, Princesses Elizabeth and Margaret Rose on the balcony at Buckingham Palace after the Coronation on 12 May 1937.

Famous portrait

The famous Norman Parkinson portrait of the late Queen Mother with The Queen and Princess Margaret was shown on a Swaziland 15c. value (487), issued on 7 June 1985 to celebrate the 'Life and Times of Queen Elizabeth The Queen Mother'.

This enchanting omnibus issue also featured stamps depicting The Queen Mother with Princess Margaret at Trooping The Colour – Mauritius 2r. (700); at Badminton Horse Trials—Solomon Islands 25c. (539) and at Ascot—Tristan da Cunha 20p (391).

Princess Margaret is included in a photograph of The Royal Family taken at Windsor Castle on Princess Elizabeth's 14th birthday on 21 April 1940 and shown on stamps by several countries including Falkland Islands Dependencies, 7p (129) 'Life and Times of Queen Elizabeth the Queen Mother', issued on 23 June 1985; British Antarctic Territory, £1 (187) 'The Queen Mother's 90th birthday', issued locally on 25 December 1990 and British Indian Ocean Territory £1 (107), issued on 4 August 1990.

The Falklands Islands 10p value in the '60th Birthday of Queen Elizabeth II' series, issued on 21 April 1986 (522), shows Princesses Elizabeth and Margaret at St Paul's, Walden Bury, Welwyn in 1932.

Princess Margaret is shown standing next to her mother, in a photograph taken outside Clarence House on 4 August 1994, The Queen Mother's 94th birthday,

used by Tristan da Cunha for the 50p value in 'The Queen Mother's Century' omnibus, issued on 18 August 1999 (659).

A Bermuda 70c. stamp (847), issued 7 August 2000, and a St Helena 25p value within a five-stamp miniature sheet (MS814) included engaging pictures of Princess Margaret to commemorate her 70th birthday on 21 August 2000.

Golden Jubilee

The Crown Agents Golden Jubilee omnibus issued on 6 February this year carries several stamps depicting Princess Margaret. They include the Norfolk Island 45c., featuring a black and white picture of HM Queen Elizabeth The Queen Mother with the Princesses Elizabeth and Margaret, taken during 1930, and a Papua New Guinea, 1k.25, showing a colour picture of The Queen Mother with the Princesses taken on 8 July 1941 in the grounds of Windsor Castle. The British Antarctic Territory 20p and Gibraltar 30p show a photograph of Princess Elizabeth making her first broadcast on 12 October 1940, accompanied by her younger sister, Princess Margaret Rose.

The Cayman Islands 30c. and St Helena 20p depict 'Princess Guides'. The Cayman Islands stamp shows a photograph of Princesses Elizabeth and Margaret wearing Girl Guide uniforms at Frogmore, Windsor, on 30 June 1942, while the St Helena stamp depicts the two Princesses in their Guide uniforms practising first aid – Princess Margaret has her arm in a sling.

Meanwhile, the Isle of Man featured Princess Margaret on the 14p value (282) in a set issued on 31 January 1985 to commemorate the 75th Anniversary of the Girl Guide Movement. Princess Margaret, the movement's President, is depicted in her Guide uniform, together with the Isle of Man standard and guides.

Princess Margaret is also shown with Prime Minister Kennedy Simmonds on a St Kitts $5 miniature sheet marking the '5th Anniversary of Independence' issued on 19 September 1988 (MS265).

Princess Margaret was frequently in the news. In a personal message from Clarence House dated 31 October 1955 she selflessly wrote: 'I have decided not to marry Group Captain Peter Townsend.... Mindful of the Church's teaching that Christian marriage is indissoluble, and conscious of my duty to the Commonwealth, I have resolved to put these considerations before any others.'

On 6 May 1960, the 120th anniversary of the Penny Black, she married Mr Anthony Armstrong-Jones, who took the title Earl of Snowdon the next year. Fiji issued a 25c. stamp on 21 April 1986 depicting The Royal Family on the balcony of Buckingham Palace after the Wedding (715). Sadly, in May 1978 Princess Margaret and Lord Snowdon announced they were to divorce.

Princess Margaret's children, Viscount David Linley (born on 3 November 1961) and Lady Sarah Armstrong-Jones (born on 1 May 1964) have both been shown on stamps, among them the South Georgia & The South Sandwich Islands 30p 'Queen Mother's Century' (290), on which they appear, together with Prince Edward, at The Queen Mother's 70th birthday on 4 August 1970.

Lady Sarah Armstrong-Jones (Lady Chatto) is also shown with Prince Edward and Princess Anne at Trooping the Colour on the Falkland Islands Dependencies 22p value (130) in the 'Life and Times of Queen Elizabeth The Queen Mother' series, issued on 23 June 1985.

On 25 February 1998, the papers reported that Princess Margaret was undergoing tests at a hospital in Barbados after suffering a mild stroke while on holiday on the Caribbean island of Mustique.

Princess Margaret's last public appearance was on the late Queen Mother's 101st birthday, 4 August 2001. She was sitting in a wheelchair and looked very frail. She died aged 71 at 6.30am on Saturday 9 February 2002 at the King Edward VII Hospital, situated across the road from the premises of the Royal Philatelic Society London at 41 Devonshire Place. The Queen's younger sister had suffered a third stroke on Friday afternoon. The funeral service took place on 15 February in St George's Chapel at Windsor Castle, where exactly 50 years earlier to the day, 15 February 1952, her father, King George VI has been laid to rest.

'A timeless reminder'

Nigel Fordham, Head of the Crown Agents Stamp Bureau said in a tribute: 'The Crown Agents are pleased to have featured HRH The Princess Margaret on stamps throughout her life. They are a timeless reminder and record of personal moments with her family as well as featuring her carrying out various public duties.'

Royal Mail has never featured, or included, Princess Margaret on a British stamp. In January 2001, while the Princess was bravely battling against serious illness, I urged Royal Mail to include her on a stamp with her sister to mark The Queen's 75th birthday on 21 April that year.

The story, put out on 14 January 2001 by Press Association, the largest news agency in the UK, drew a negative response from Royal Mail. A spokesman said: 'We have no plans to issue a stamp featuring Princess Margaret or commemorating the Queen's 75th birthday.'

Perhaps Royal Mail will now find a reason to issue a stamp featuring stamp collector Princess Margaret. I have little confidence that it will. However, Business Post, the Birmingham-based company poised to challenge Royal Mail's postal monopoly, collecting and sorting business post, has requested permission from Buckingham Palace to put the Queen's head on its first private stamps. If granted, I'm sure the firm would be delighted to include a photograph of HM The Queen and her sister on one of its first private stamps.

70th Birthday Stamps for HM The Queen—The Crown Agents issue

Hugh Jefferies looks at the background to 'Royal' birthday stamps and visits the Crown Agents to find out how a modern omnibus series is produced

Royal Birthdays have become a popular subject for stamp issues in recent years. The first Commonwealth territory to hit on the idea was Newfoundland, who issued a 4c. stamp in 1947 for the then Princess Elizabeth's 21st birthday.

Elsewhere in the world Royal birthday stamps were already well established. Sweden had issued a set for the 70th birthday of King Gustav V in 1928, followed by sets for his 80th and 90th birthdays in 1938 and 1948. His son, King Gustav VI Adolf had a 70th birthday set in 1952 and 80th, 85th and 90th birthday issues in 1962, 1967 and 1972. The present King, Carl XVI Gustav saw his first birthday issue in 1986, on the occasion of his 40th, while a 1993 issue combined the commemoration of Queen Silvia's 50th birthday and the 20th anniversary of King Carl Gustav's accession to the throne.

Several other countries have also adopted royal birthdays as subjects for stamp issues, although the birthdays which have been celebrated have not always been as obvious as those of Sweden. Afghanistan commemorated King Mohammed Zahir Shah's 46th birthday in 1960, his 49th, 50th and 51st birthdays in 1963, 1964 and 1965 and his 55th, 56th, 57th and 58th birthdays in 1969, 1970, 1971 and 1972. He was deposed before he reached his 59th birthday so we do not know if the series had been expected to be continuous from then on.

Commonwealth countries, however, did not follow the precedent set by Newfoundland until 1980 when 30 territories, including Great Britain, issued stamps commemorating the 80th birthday of HM Queen Elizabeth the Queen Mother. Most issues consisted of single stamps with the total amounting to only 41 stamps and 12 miniature sheets.

1980 also saw the first of what has become a regular issue celebrating the Queen's birthday by Australia.

Life and times

The 85th birthday of the Queen Mother was celebrated in 1985 by a series of stamps entitled 'The Life and Times of Queen Elizabeth the Queen Mother'. The stamps of the Commonwealth countries involved totalled 262 with 47 miniature sheets. The following year, for the Queen's 60th birthday, 233 stamps and 28 miniature sheets were issued, including two *se-tenant* pairs by Great Britain.

By 1990 and the Queen Mother's 90th birthday things seem to have calmed down, with 40 countries, again including Great Britain, contributing 119 stamps and 19 miniature sheets—a figure that would have been a lot lower had it not been for the 27 stamps from the Grenadines of St Vincent.

In 1991 33 territories combined the 65th birthday of the Queen with the 70th birthday of Prince Philip in an omnibus totalling 85 stamps and 11 sheets, while the stamp issues for the 95th birthday of the Queen Mother were but a fraction of those issued for her 85th.

Months and months in advance

In spite of the reducing numbers of stamps involved, one might have supposed that the precedent had been set—there would clearly be an omnibus issue for the Queen's 70th birthday. I was therefore very pleasantly surprised to find out that, certainly so far as the Crown Agents were concerned, an issue of this nature is only recommended after very careful consideration and discussion. In fact many countries made their final decision to participate towards the end of 1995, after their stamp issue programmes for 1996 had been set.

Considerable variation

The nature of the relationship between the Crown Agents and the countries whose stamps they handle (their 'principals') varies quite considerably. In some cases the CA acts as a wholesaler in the UK, but has no involvement in stamp design and production. Many countries, however, provide detailed instructions to the Crown Agents as to the stamps which they wish to issue but rely on the expertise of the CA to arrange their design, printing and distribution, while others rely also upon the Crown Agents themselves to make recommendations as to their issuing programme.

As far as omnibus issues are concerned, the Crown Agents regularly consult collectors and the stamp trade as to what topics would be popular and it was following such a consultation process that it was decided to propose to the countries which they serve that they issue stamps to celebrate the Queen's birthday.

48 countries were circulated with the suggestion but, owing to the fact that many of them had already decided on their issuing programmes, only ten have responded positively.

Meanwhile the Crown Agents commissioned one of their most talented and prolific artists, Derek Miller, to come up with some design ideas and four different design roughs were submitted to the Palace. This is the normal procedure for any stamps which include either the Queen's head or the Royal Cypher in the design, although normally the Crown Agents' advice is accepted without discussion. On this occasion, however, Her Majesty the Queen took an active interest in the issue from the start, resulting in the acceptance of a series of designs, as recommended by the Crown Agents Stamp Bureau, featuring photographs of the Queen with, in the foreground, a view of the country concerned, thus reinforcing Her Majesty's link with

Two rejected designs

Rejected designs in sheetlet form. The scraperboard design between the stamps was used on the issued souvenir sheets

each as Head of the Commonwealth. The photographs were all supplied by Alpha of London and have been taken within the last five years.

'An engraved look'

Meanwhile acceptances were coming in from the territories either for a straight set of four stamps or for a set of four plus a miniature sheet featuring, in the border, a floral 'scraperboard' design which had been included in one of the alternative designs; in the words of Derek Miller, 'to give an "engraved" look' to the stamps.

Commissioning the printers

As the design work was being completed, with a different photograph of the Queen being selected for every stamp, the Crown Agents set about commissioning the printers to produce them. Four different printers have been involved; BDT International Security Printing Ltd of Dublin, Cartor SA of France, Joh Enschedé en Zonen of the Netherlands and Walsall Security Printers Ltd; all using the lithographic process. Each country's work is individually tendered for by the printers while the territory concerned will often express a preference for the printing method and paper to be used.

To achieve a common issue date in each territory, priority has to be given to the stamps of those territories which are most difficult to supply. The Queen's birthday falls on 21 April; this being a Sunday, when the post offices in most territories will be closed, most will be issuing the stamps on Monday 22 April. Pitcairn Islands, however, where most of the population are Seventh Day Adventists, can issue its stamps on the birthday itself as the post office is open on Sundays.

Problems

In order to get the stamps to Tristan da Cunha before the date of issue, they had to be flown to Cape Town by 8 February in order to be shipped to Tristan on board the supply ship *Hekla*, while supplying new issues to Pitcairn Islands and the British Antarctic Territory present their own problems (see panel alongside).

For most territories these days, however, shipping the stamps by air in time to meet the issue date is less of a problem than it must have been in the past.

I left the Crown Agents aware that there was much more to stamp production than printing a few pretty miniature pictures and supplying them to stamp dealers for sale to collectors. The whole process from initial concept, 'selling' the idea to the territories concerned, commissioning the designs and gaining approval for the designs, placing the printing contract and then shipping the stamps in order for them to be on sale on the due date requires a great deal of planning and organisation. It is no surprise that, as usual, the result is a set of stamps pleasing to the eye and reasonable in cost—a credit to the dedicated and enthusiastic team at the Crown Agents Stamp Bureau.

The artist

Derek Miller is a full time stamp artist who has been responsible for some 4000 designs from 75 different countries.

He began work in advertising; designing advertisements and brochures, where he developed his skills in visualising, illustrating, retouching and producing finished artwork. His involvement in stamp design resulted from a period in which he shared offices with a photographer who 'happened

to be photographer to the Crown Agents Stamp Bureau', preparing photographs of stamp artwork, and who would occasionally 'pop in asking if I could "change this value or that line of lettering"'. It was not long before he was asked to design a set of stamps himself.

Some commissions come direct from postal administrations and security printers but most of his work comes from agents. He has designed eight omnibus series prior to the new Queen's 70th birthday issue; including those for the tercentenary of Lloyds of London and the 20th anniversary of the first manned moon landing. It is with royal events, however, that his work has become most closely associated, having designed stamps for the 1986 Royal Wedding, HRH The Queen Mother's 90th birthday in 1990, the Queen's 65th and Prince Philip's 70th birthdays in 1991 and the 40th anniversary of the accession.

Derek Miller's designs are not confined to royal portraits though. As a glance through the stamp catalogue will show, buildings, butterflies, ships, birds and a whole host of other subjects which have appeared in our stamp albums over the past decade or more have originated in his studio.

A hazardous process

Pitcairn only receives three supply ships each year so it was very important that the stamps reached Auckland in time for the due departure date. Had they missed the supply ship it would have been necessary to persuade a ship en-route for South America to take a one-day detour to Pitcairn. Even then it would not have stopped but just slowed down and dropped off its cargo in watertight containers for collection by longboat, a hazardous process which has resulted in injury in the past. On one or two occasions stamp supplies have even been parachuted on to the island by the Royal New Zealand Air Force—so perhaps the odd crease or dent in a Pitcairn Islands stamp might be excused!

Delivering stamps to Pitcairn

When it comes to shipping first day covers out of Pitcairn, on the other hand, the supply ship is the only option—which is why it takes such a long time for covers and used stamps from Pitcairn and Tristan da Cunha to reach collectors in the UK.

Impossible

British Antarctic Territory is, of course, even more isolated. For several months during the Antarctic winter it is impossible to get supplies to the scientists and technicians of the British Antarctic Survey for whom the stamps are issued. The four main bases, Halley, Rothera, Signy and Fossil Bluff, are linked to the outside world by two BAS ships, the *Bransfield* and the *James Clark Ross*. Stamps can only be delivered and first day covers despatched twice a year when the ships call—which is why the British Antarctic Territory set is not being issued until November.

Artwork for accepted design (above) and issued stamps

The full list of stamps included in the Crown Agents omnibus series commemorating the 70th birthday of Her Majesty Queen Elizabeth is as follows:

Ascension Island: 20p, 25p, 30p, 65p
British Antarctic Territory: to be decided
British Indian Ocean Territory: 20p, 24p, 30p, 56p plus a £1 Souvenir Sheet
British Virgin Islands: 10c., 30c., 45c., $1.50 plus a $2 Souvenir Sheet
Falkland Islands: 17p, 40p, 45p, 65p plus a £1 Souvenir Sheet
Pitcairn Islands: 20c., 90c., $1.80, $3
St Helena: 15p, 25p, 53p, 60p plus a £1.50 Souvenir Sheet
Samoa: 70s., 90s., $1, $3 plus a $5 Souvenir Sheet
Tokelau: 40c., $1, $1.25, $2 plus a $3 Souvenir Sheet
Tristan da Cunha: 15p, 20p, 45p, 60p

ROYAL BIRTHDAY

A review of the stamps depicting Queen Elizabeth II

Daniel O'Connor Cooke

NPM card SS37 showing the Dorothy Wilding portrait of The Queen — see page 51 for more details.

It is said that Queen Elizabeth II is the most photographed women in the world. Not only is The Queen photographed but her likeness is sculptured, drawn, engraved, painted and moulded in all types of materials, not always doing true justice either to her beauty or personality. That, perhaps, is a draw back to being born to public duty. As Princess Elizabeth of York she first appeared on a stamp in 1932 — a Newfoundland issue (S.G. 214) and now at the time of her sixtieth birthday celebration, it is estimated that she has appeared on stamps issued by no less than 115 postal authorities around the world.

No one could estimate just how many people on this planet have actually seen The Queen on her countless national and international tours or how many might recognise her likeness. The British monarch has been a symbol of our country on our postage stamps since they began in 1840 and we have never needed to use the words 'Great Britain'. However, the British Post Office was very slow to portray members of the Royal Family other than the reigning sovereign and it was not until 1937 that Queen Elizabeth (The Queen Mother) was the first consort to appear on a British stamp on the Coronation issue of that year (S.G. 461).

Stamps showing Princess Elizabeth

On the other hand her daughter, Princess Elizabeth (of York) had already appeared on the Newfoundland stamp, mentioned above, one of a set which included one showing her 'Uncle David' as Prince of Wales (S.G. 212), later to become King Edward VIII. The Commonwealth countries were way ahead of GB in using portraits of Royal children in addition to those of the sovereign. The Princesses Elizabeth and Margaret appeared on the stamps of several countries during the reign of their father King George VI. After her debut on the Newfoundland stamp; Princess Elizabeth appeared on a Canadian stamp in 1935 as part of a set issued to commemorate the Silver Jubilee of her grandfather King George V (S.G. 335). The young, and ever popular, princess would again appear on stamps of Newfoundland in 1938 (S.G. 270,279), Canada for the Royal Visit of 1939 (372); New Zealand for the Health issues of 1943 (637) and 1944 (663-4), the

1946 – 7 Peace issues of New Zealand (670) and Southern Rhodesia (66), the 1947 Royal Visits issues of Basutoland [Lesotho] (34-5), Bechuanaland [Botswana] (134-5), South Africa (113), Southern Rhodesia [Zimbabwe] (63) and South West Africa [Namibia] (136), her twenty-first birthday issue of Newfoundland (293) her wedding issue of Australia (222) and Canada (410) and, finally, Malta which issued three stamps to mark her visit there in 1950 (255-7). No less than ten issuing authorities has used the likeness of the young Princess Elizabeth but these did not include GB!

As Her Majesty Queen Majesty II

It was not until she became Queen that she was to appear on a British stamp. This was to be the definitive issues of December 1952, ten months after her accession, when the Dorothy Wilding portrait was used on the 1½d. and 2½d. denominations (S.G. 517, 519). It had been at the beginning of her tour of Kenya with the Duke of Edinburgh that the dreadful and sudden news of her father's death was broken to her and the realisation that having left London a Princess she was to return immediately as Queen and Sovereign.

This twenty-five year old wife and mother had been devoted to both her parents who had weathered the storm of the abdication of Edward VIII; were thrust upon the Throne and within three years found themselves amid the horrors of the Second World War. All this took its toll upon King George but towards the end of his reign he was to enjoy the wedding of his elder daughter to Lieutenant Philip Mountbatten (former Prince of Greece and Denmark) and the birth of his grandchildren — Prince Charles in 1948 and Princess Anne in 1950. In 1951, the last full year of his reign, he presided over the Festival of Britain which, it turned out, was to mark the eve of 'The New Elizabethan Era'.

The Coronation Commemorative Issues

Seventy-eight Commonwealth postal authorities issued at least one stamp each to mark the 1953 Coronation. GB issued four stamps (S.G. 532-5) which were also used with appropriate overprints in the British administrations in North Africa and Arabia. Three of the

stamps used the popular Dorothy Wilding portrait with symbols of the realm, but by far the most attractive was the 1s.3d. value (S.G. 534). This was the work of Edmund Dulac who pre-empted the moment of crowning by drawing a full face of The Queen wearing the St Edward Crown, made for the coronation of Charles II in 1661 and only worn by the monarch for the actual crowning ceremony. Although obviously printed well in advance, the stamps were not released in Britain until 3 June as Coronation Day (2 June) was a public holiday with festivities and street parties across the land.

The vast majority of Commonwealth countries used an 'omnibus' design with only the country name, currency and colour differing — see for example Cyprus S.G. 172. The principle design of this stamp was the photograph of The Queen wearing her favourite 'light tiara' which had been a gift from her grandmother Queen Mary. The 'omnibus' issue was designed and engraved by Bradbury Wilkinson & Co. and recess printed by De La Rue & Co. The same photograph was used in differing designs by South West Africa (S.G. 149–53), another but with the same tiara by Southern Rhodesia (77) and South Africa (143) reverted to the Dorothy Wilding photograph in which Her Majesty wears the royal diadem made originally for George IV and now particularly associated with the Queen's annual drive to the Palace of Westminster for the State Opening of Parliament.

The Great Occasion

Apart from the Coronation regalia illustrated within the designs of the British issues and the 'advance' portrait by Dulac of a Crowned Queen, very little of the pomp and circumstance of the occasion could be gleaned from the 1953 stamps. The issues of New Zealand (S.G. 714–8) and Samoa (229–30) did show the exterior of Westminster Abbey and the Coronation Coach but we had to wait twenty-four years to see much of the magnificent detail on stamps.

In 1977 many of the stamps issued for the Silver Jubilee of The Queen's Accession used modern printing techniques to illustrate the full splendour of the Coronation. By travelling the philatelic world we can follow the events of that happy and memorable day. It was a time when the vast majority of homes did not possess a TV and an estimated one million loyal subjects and visitors lined the streets of London to pay their own humble homage to the Second Elizabeth. Many thousands had slept rough, not discouraged by damp June weather. They were well rewarded by the gradual build up of military personnel from all over the Commonwealth before the climax of the morning — The Queen's Procession leaving Buckingham Palace. Earlier that morning The Queen had received the exciting news of the conquest of Mount Everest by (Sir) Edmund Hilary on 29 May.

None of the many dignitaries in the procession won the hearts of the people so quickly as Queen Salote on Tonga. This tall and striking lady (who had succeeded to her Polynesian throne thirty-five years earlier) was seen in an open carriage smiling broadly through the heavy rain which in her native Friendly Islands is always considered a blessing from heaven (Tonga S.G. 598–602).

Anticipation and excitement mounted in both London and all around the world as people tuned in their 'wirelesses' and crowded around the small number of television sets for the first ever televised coronation. Panic occurred within the BBC when it was discovered that their mains supply to the Abbey had failed, fortunately it was restored within minutes of the scheduled broadcast.

The Silver Jubilee issue of Belize (S.G. 451) shows The Queen supported by the Bishops of Durham and Bath and Wells and attended by her six Maids of Honour. After the Recognition in the 'Theatre' of the Abbey the Queen sat in the Chair of Estate (Bermuda S.G. 373) for the taking of the Oath (British Antarctic Territory

S.G. 85). The Presentation of The Holy Bible (British Virgin Islands 366) was followed by the Annointing (Falklands 327). Having moved across to King Edward's Chair (made in 1301) The Queen was presented with the Regalia (Mauritius 518) followed by the climatic and emotive Crowning (Montserrat 398). At that moment the Royal Dukes, Princesses, Peers and Peeresses placed their own coronets upon their heads to show that 'The Crown is fount of all honours' and then they paid homage. The St Helena 26p stamp (S.G. 334) shows the Duke of Edinburgh paying homage to his wife and Sovereign and the Archbishop and Bishops are shown on the St Christopher Nevis Anguilla $1.50 stamp (369).

In 1973 the Cook Islands markd the twentieth anniversary of the Coronation — the 10c. stamp (s.g. 429) shows the famous Cecil Beaton photograph of The Queen wearing the Imperial State Crown and holding the Orb and Sceptre. (During the Coronation ceremony the Imperial State Crown was exchanged for the heavier St Edward Crown which was left in the St Edward's Chapel). A splendid profile protrait is shown on the Turks & Caicos Islands 25c. stamp (S.G. 473). The return to the Palace is shown on Swaziland 25c. (269) and the Balcony Appearance of the whole Royal Family on the $1 stamp of Aitutaki (228).

Four-and-a-half year old Prince Charles had been taken to the Abbey for the moment of the Crowning but two-and-a-half year old Princess Anne had remained at Buckingham Palace watching the TV until The Queen's return. Prince Charles had already appeared on New Zealand stamps — with his mother in 1950 (S.G. 701–2) and on his own in 1952 (711). The 1952 New Zealand set also showed Princess Anne (710) and she appeared with The Queen on the Silver Jubilee 45c. stamps of Dominica (593).

Royal Tours

The 1952 Tour had been curtailed by the death of George VI but The Queen was determined to visit her Dominions and Colonies as soon as possible. It was a wrench to leave their children but The Queen and the Duke left London on the evening of 23 November 1953 to travel over 43,000 miles in just five-and-a-half months. Some of the exotic sights which the Royal Couple saw on route are illustrated on stamps issued for the visits which also carried The Queen's portrait. Bermuda was the first host country (S.G. 151) and onto Jamaica (154) and Panama. Fiji's stamp showed their Coat of Arms and the Wilding portrait of The Queen (279). Queen Salote was host in Tonga and Christmas and New Year were spent in New Zealand which issued two stamps — one of The Queen and one of the Royal Couple (721–2).

Australia issued similar stamps for the visit in January 1954 (272–4). Onto the Cocos Islands and a leisurely cruise to Ceylon [Sri Lanka] with its elephants (434), to Aden (73) and Uganda (KUT 166). The Queen and the Duke visited Libya briefly on 1 May and arrived in Malta on 3 May to be met by Lord Louis Mountbatten (India S.G. 978). Lord and Lady Mountbatten had brought the Royal Children to Malta to be reunited with their parents before the final journey home via Gibraltar (S.G. 159).

Not surprisingly The Queen did not go abroad again for over a year, and then for a 'family' State Visit to 'Uncle' King Olav in Norway. The Queen has, however, travelled the world extensively throughout her thirty-four year reign and the majority of countries do not mark state visits with special stamp issues. Ironically The Queen has appeared on stamps of several countries which might today find the issue embarrassing. Iran used the Wilding portrait along with that of the Shah on two stamps for the Queen's State Visit there in 1961 (S.G. 1223–4). The controversial but very successful visit to Ghana later that year was commemorated with a set of three

52

stamps showing The Queen and a map of Africa (271-3). The special air mail stamps of Ethiopia in 1965 showed The Queen and Emperor Haile Selassie marking her visit there (601-3).

It is now less usual for Commonwealth countries to use The Queen's portrait on their stamps — but even republics within the organisation have shown their great respect by continuing to honour her with special issues for Royal anniversaries and visits.

Stamp portraits of The Queen

It is a possible but daunting task to plot the first sixty years of The Queen's life through stamp issues.

Everyone has his or her favourite stamp. It would be impossible in an article such as this to mention even a quarter of all the stamps showing formal or informal portraits of The Queen. Numerous countries have used some very attractive portraits. Australia has used a great variety including those for the Royal Visit of 1963 (348-9) and the 1980 Birthday stamp (741). The latter was the first of what is now an annual issue but the British Post Office will be setting a precedent this month by issuing birthday commemoratives for a reigning monarch. (The only other Royal birthday stamp marked the Queen Mother's 80th birthday in 1980 — S.G. 1129).

A new portrait of The Queen with the Duke did appear on the British stamps issued for their Silver Wedding in 1972 (916-7) and one of their actual wedding portraits appeared on the Cook Islands 1c. Royal Visit stamp of 1971 (S.G. 345). The more popular British design is that using Arnold Machin's plaster cast — particularly well featured on the 1969 and 1970-2 high value definitives (S.G. 787-90, 829-31a). The Channel Islands and the Isle of Man have been more adventurous, the most attractive being from Jersey — for example the 1969 1s.9d. and £1 definitives (S.G. 25, 29), the 1977 £2 (155, and the 1983 £5 (271). The Annigoni portrait was used by The Gambia for the Royal Visit stamps in 1961 (186-9) and in 1962 Hong Kong used it on its definitives (196-210), it has featured on other Commonwealth stamps in the ensuing years.

Some other striking portraits can be found on Cook Islands 1963 1s.6d. (S.G. 170), Grenada 1966 $2 (244), Malta 1967 Royal Visit 4d. (397), Tristan da Cunha 1967 10s. and £1 (84a-b), Brazil 1968 70c. Royal Visit (1235), Canada 1973 Royal Visit (759-60), New Zealand 1974 NZ Day 4c. (MS 1046) and 1977 Jubilee set (MS 1137), Penrhyn 1977 Jubilee $2 (102) and the 1983 Caribbean Visits to the Cayman Islands 1 (572) and Jamaica $2 (573).

The Peter Grugeon portrait can be found on the Canada 1977 Jubilee issue (855), Fiji 1982 Royal Visit (645), Falklands 1983 150th Anniversary £2 (449), and Barbuda 1984 Royal Family series $1 (713). A new Camera Press photograph was used on the 25c. and 35c. definitives of New Zealand issued in July 1985 (S.G. 1370-1).

The British stamps commemorating Her Majesty's Sixtieth Birthday this month show The Queen at different ages and the vast majority of us are delighted that the Post Office is paying such a worthy tribute.

St Helena commemorated the Silver Jubilee with a reminder of The Queen's visit in 1947 with her parents and her sister Princess Margaret (S.G. 332) and in 1961 issued a £1 definitive showing The Queen with her baby son Prince Andrew (189) — whose own visit there in 1984 was also marked by special stamps (436-7). The Kenya Jubilee issue shows The Queen and the Duke back in 1952 before their peace was shattered at Sagana Royal Lodge (S.G. 91). Her Majesty in military uniform, for Trooping The Colour on her Official Birthday, is shown on New Zealand high values of 1953-8 (S.G. 733b-6), Fiji 1962 3d. (313) and Guernsey 1981 Royal Wedding 25p

(238). The Tristan da Cunha 1974 Churchill Centenary 25p (194) shows The Queen arriving at 10 Downing Street to dine with Sir Winston upon the eve of his retirement in April 1955. The Barbados Silver Jubilee 15c. shows Her Majesty knighting Gary Sobers at Bridgetown (574) and the Hong Kong Silver Jubilee $1.30 shows their Queen painting the eye of The Dragon during her visit to the colony in 1975 (362).

Sixtieth Birthday Issues

Great Britain and many Commonwealth countries will be issuing stamps to commemorate the Queen's sixtieth birthday. Britain's issue, on 21 April — the actual birth date — consists of two *se-tenant* pairs designed by Jeffery Matthews, who has been responsible for several previous 'Royal' issues. Each pair shows six portraits of the Queen spanning the six decades since her birth — at age two (1928), in army uniform, age sixteen (1942), the famous Wilding portrait (1952) a balcony scene in uniform (1958), an informal portrait taken at Badminton (1973) and a formal portrait (1982). A special Souvenir Book containing illustrations and background material, as well as the stamps, is also to be issued.

The Channel Islands are also issuing special stamps on 21 April. From Guernsey come four stamps depicting scenes from Royal visits to the Bailwick — Princess Elizabeth and the Duke of Edinburgh riding in a horse-drawn carriage in Sark (1949), The Queen leaving the Royal Court House, St Peter Port (1957), The Queen receiving a gift of traditional Guernsey sweaters from the Guernsey Island Federation of Women's Institutes (1957) and a special sitting of the Court of Chief Pleas, Beau Sejour, St Peter Port (1978). Jersey's special stamp, a £1 value showing a portrait of Her Majesty, will later become part of the island's definitives series.

The Isle of Man celebrates two Royal birthdays with its special issue, that of the Queen and the sixty-fifth of the Duke of Edinburgh. In the form of two decorative stamp sheetlets, one containing six double-size stamps featuring the Royal couple together, the other six *se-tenant* pairs showing individual portraits of the couple. The sheetlets are to be issued on 28 August.

From the Commonwealth twenty-four territories under the wing of the Crown Agents — Ascension, Bahamas, Barbados, Bermuda, Cayman Islands, Fiji, Falkland Islands, Hong Kong, Jamaica, Kiribati, Mauritius, Norfolk Island, Papua New Guinea, Pitcairn Islands, St Helena, Samoa, Seychelles, Solomon Islands, South Georgia & South Sandwich Islands, Swaziland, Tristan da Cunha, Vanuatu, Zambia and Zil Elwannyen Sesel — are each to issue five stamps designed by Tony Theobald. Each country's stamps will adhere to the following pattern: the lowest value will depict a black and white photograph of the Queen from her birth in 1926 to her accession in 1952, the next value features a colour photograph of an event in Her Majesty's life from her accession to the present day, the middle value illustrates a Royal visit to the issuing country or Her Majesty fulfilling various roles as Head of State, the fourth value illustrates a modern portrait of the Queen, the final value, common to all countries, shows a photograph of the Queen visiting the Crown Agents Head Office in London in 1983, to celebrate the Agents 150th anniversary. Each printed sheet comprises fifty stamps separated into two panes of twenty-five by a vertical gutter in which are depicted an order of chivalry, a Royal residence, a birthday greeting, an insignia of a unit of the British Army of which the Queen is Commander-in-Chief and the issuing country's coat of arms.

Let us with Her Majesty many more Happy and Glorious years. God Save The Queen!

ROYAL WEDDING POSTCARDS

Valerie Monahan

In Edwardian times picture postcards were well placed among the mass-produced parade of souvenirs to commemorate Coronations and Royal Jubilees. There were also plenty of photocards around to record the nuptials of foreign Royalty — even to the showing of the wedding cake made for Princess Ena of Battenberg when she married the King of Spain. But there were no picture postcard chronicles of a British Royal Wedding until 1922.

Ideas for picture postal cards were still at the 'idle chat' stage when the lovely Princess Alexandra of Denmark joined the Prince of Wales at the altar of St George's Chapel, Windsor on 10 March, 1863. And when, some thirty years later, their son the Duke of York married Princess Victoria Mary of Teck on 6 July, 1893 in the Chapel Royal, St James's Palace, there was still a year to go before the picture postcard was to make its modest debut. A reproduction, however, of 'the only authentic photograph' of part of the Wedding group for this particular Royal couple was to appear some forty-two years later. For the Silver Jubilee celebrations of their reign as T.M. King George V and Queen Mary, several sets of postcards were produced by different publishers, but the inclusion of the early Wedding photograph was due to the enterprise of W. & D. Downey, Ebury Street, London.

This was not the first time a Royal Wedding had been given commemorative postcard treatment several decades after the actual event. In 1900, when Raphael Tuck and Sons Ltd, were planning their superb 'Empire' series of cards, they managed to slip in a special reminder to note the idyllic marriage between Queen Victoria and Prince Albert at the Chapel Royal, St James's, on 10 February, 1840.

It was not until 28 February, 1922 before the first 'on the spot' British Royal Wedding Postcards appeared. The publication of these cards also coincided with a break in the Royal tradition of holding Royal Wedding ceremonies within the privacy of the Chapels Royal. A happy decision for the large band of delighted commoners who lined the route to watch the Royal Wedding procession wend its way along The Mall, through Admiralty Arch, and down Whitehall to the more commodious Westminster Abbey where The Princess Royal was married to Viscount Lascelles. The official cards to note this wedding were photographed by Vandyk Ltd, and published by J. Beagles & Co Ltd, and by the sight of them, it would appear that the happiness of the occasion was not to be revealed by smiling faces. Solemn, to the point of glumness the bride and groom stand stiffly to attention surrounded either by their respective parents or by their equally grim-faced attendants.

A year later, there came another treat for Royal Wedding spectators and collectors of Royalty postcards when the Duke of York and the delectable Lady Elizabeth Bowes-Lyon plighted their troth to each other on 26 April, 1923. This time, Elliott & Fry Ltd, were chosen to photograph the postcards for Beagles, and on one of these cards at least, a sunny smile can be seen on the face of one of the young bridesmaids, The Hon. Cecilia Bowes-Lyon. On that joyous day, no one could have predicted that some fourteen years later the destiny of this especially loved and respected Royal couple would carry them along the same route to Westminster Abbey where they were to be crowned T.M. King George VI and Queen Elizabeth.

A whole decade was to pass before the promise of another State occasion in the form of a Royal Wedding blazoned across the front pages of the newspapers. H.R.H. The Duke of Kent had fallen in love with a Princess whose beauty and elegance was so breathtaking she immediately captured the hearts of the British people — and the imagination of fashion designers. For her betrothal pictures, Princess Marina of Greece had worn a dress in a unique shade of blue which was something between turquoise and aquamarine. In no time at all the

department stores and the dress shops of Britain were doing a roaring trade selling clothes which sported this newly created colour — dubbed by the fashion world as 'Marina' blue. There was also a glimpse of a more relaxed atmosphere unfolding when it came to the publication of postcards. The Excel series produced a betrothal card entitled 'The Royal Lovers and the Family Group' in which the Royal couple and their parents are snapped arm in arm — an unusually informal pose for Royalty at that time. There were also some excellent sets of Royal Wedding postcards published by Raphael Tuck and Sons Ltd, and Valentine & Sons Ltd, of Dundee. One of the best cards to commemorate that fairy-tale wedding day on 29 November, 1934 was photographed by Bassano for Valentine's of the 'Official Wedding Group taken in Buckingham Palace', where in the bottom right corner can be seen a young Princess Elizabeth in her bridesmaid's dress.

Sadly, the wedding between Princess Marina and the Duke of Kent was to be the last to be held at Westminster Abbey for many years, for although the full pageantry of an Abbey wedding was being planned for the following year for the marriage between the Duke of Gloucester and Lady Alice Montagu-Douglas-Scott, the plans had to be cancelled due to the death of the bride's father the Duke of Buccleuch. The wedding took place quietly on 6 November, 1935 in the privacy of the Royal Chapel at Buckingham Palace.

Twelve traumatic years went by before the crowds were to assemble for an all-night sitting along the route to Westminster Abbey in readiness to witness the next Royal Wedding procession. During those intervening years, the postcard scene had been dappled with the joy of the Silver Jubilee of King George V and Queen Mary, the sadness of the processional cards depicting the funeral cortège of King George V, the excitement and delight engendered by the Coronation of King George VI and Queen Elizabeth, and the horror of a Second World War. But on 10 July, 1947 there came a warm shaft of sunlight to pierce the gloom in the form of the announcement that H.R.H. The Princess Elizabeth was engaged to be married to Lieutenant Philip Mountbatten R.N. and for the first time on postcards the human happiness of Royalty was allowed to be seen when Tuck's issued the Royal Betrothal cards. There was no mistaking the radiance of the smiles caught by a photographer from *The Times*. On the eve of 20 November, 1947 the Royal Wedding route seemed to be crammed with as many of the British public and overseas visitors as could manage to squeeze into the smallest of spaces. Nothing was going to mar the gladness of this day — not even the austerity of those post-war years. Using the sparse materials available to them, the souvenir makers and the postcard manufacturers made sure that there were enough special

---

Illustrated on page 71: Reproduction of a wedding photograph of T.M. King George V and Queen Mary — included in the Silver Jubilee set produced by W. & D. Downey, London. Cards published by J. Beagles & Co. Ltd for the wedding of The Princess Royal to Viscount Lascelles, 28 February 1922 and for the wedding of The Duke of York to the Lady Elizabeth Bowes-Lyon, 26 April 1924. Royal betrothal card published by Excel Postcards to commemorate the engagement between the Duke of Kent and the Princess Marina. Postcard No. 12 published by Raphael Tuck & Sons Ltd of the bridal pair Princess Marina and the Duke of Kent. One of the Raphael Tuck & Sons Ltd cards to commemorate the royal betrothal between The Princess Elizabeth and Lieutenant Philip Mountbatten, R.N. Anonymously published but excellently photographed card of the royal wedding between Princess Margaret and Mr Antony Armstrong-Jones. A royal betrothal card to commemorate the engagement between Princess Anne and Captain Mark Phillips — published by Charles Skilton & Fry Ltd.

Royal Wedding Postcards

Royal Wedding Postcards

keepsakes to satisfy a public eager to have some reminder that although the British economy may have been battered Britain was by no means beaten when it came to sharing this particular Royal joy.

Just the same, the postcards issued to mark the engagement and Royal Wedding Day of Princess Elizabeth brought to a close the major part of the postcard producing industry. Many of the famous names in the publishing world abandoned postcards in favour of producing folded greetings cards, and those who continued to soldier on confined their efforts to the safety of continental-sized viewcards and the perennial favourites of holiday-makers, the saucy seaside comics. As it happened this policy paid off, for despite the interest in actually collecting postcards having been abandoned during the post-war years up to the mid-sixties, picture cards slotted into the convenient if unexceptonal form of brief communication, and as every postcard publisher knew, there would always be a ready market for cards which described Royal occasions — with or without the assistance of collectors.

The machinery was set into motion for the production of cards to describe the Coronation of H.M. Queen Elizabeth II on 2 June, 1953, and seven years later for the marriage of Princess Margaret to Mr Antony. Armstrong-Jones at Westminster Abbey on 6 May, 1960. In addition to the superb photographic cards published to commemorate the Royal Wedding of Princess Margaret, there were many delightful souvenir examples with more adventurous themes such as silvered backgrounds to impressionist drawings of The Mall festively decorated for the occasion.

But by the time it was announced that Princess Anne was to be married to Captain Mark Phillips 14 November, 1973, the postcard publishing concerns were just beginning to awaken to the fact that not only had a revival for collecting postcards been steadily growing around them since the late sixties, but that the hobby, once considered to be nothing more than a frivolous Edwardian craze, was fast becoming a serious institution poised to take its place with the more traditional collecting pursuits. True, the day of the modern postcard had not yet arrived, but there were many far-sighted people who gathered in the coloured cards published to commemorate the Royal Betrothal and Wedding Day cards of Princes Anne.

And so to that February day earlier this year when the engagement between H.R.H. The Prince of Wales and Lady Diana Spencer was announced to bring a much needed splash of colour into the lives of the British people — and a glimmer of hope to brighten the face of British industry.

Within days of that long-awaited announcement the souvenir industries were forging ahead with plans to make and market a huge variety of commemorative items, and the tourist agencies — and entrepreneurs — were busy with their schemes to attract an influx of overseas visitors to Britain during Royal Wedding week. There was no shilly-shallying around on the postcard front either. Veldale Covers of Kidderminster, Worcestershire, and Michael Dummer in his Carousel range brought out limited editions of Royal Betrothal cards before the first week in March was out. J. Salmon Ltd of Sevenoaks, Kent published a delightful coloured photograph of the Royal couple with the date of the marriage 29 July, 1981 printed on the address side. Charles Skilton & Fry Ltd produced a delectable trio of eminently collectable cards which includes the enchanting photograph by Lord Snowdon of Lady Diana. And the first of the Royal Wedding commemoratives designed by Faga with the date 29 July, 1981 printed on the front over the inscription, 'The Marriage of The Prince of Wales & Lady Diana Spencer' was available to collectors by April. Copies of all these cards can be purchased from Ron Griffiths, 47 Long Arrotts, Hemel Hempstead, Herts — for apart from the Salmon's and Charles Skilton cards, few of the limited edition types are on public sale in the shops.

This choice of Royal Betrothal cards gives a fine start to building up a small album of Royal Wedding cards, for it can be guaranteed that this particular celebration will attract a great deal of postcard attention — especially as the route has been diverted from Westminster Abbey to St Paul's Cathedral!

Illustrations: Two cards from the trio published by Charles Skilton & Fry Ltd to commemorate the engagement of The Prince of Wales to Lady Diana Spencer — including the enchanting photographic portrait of Lady Diana by Lord Snowdon — and a card designed by Faga.

A ROYAL YEAR IN POSTMARKS

John Holman

For collectors who specialise in stamps and postmarks connected with Royalty, 1981 has clearly been an *annus mirabilis*. The engagement of the Prince of Wales to Lady Diana Spencer was announced from Buckingham Palace on 24 February (the opening day of STAMPEX) and the wedding took place at St Paul's Cathedral amid all the splendour associated with such occasions on 29 July. The Post Office commemorated the marriage with two stamps issued a week before the ceremony and no fewer than 20 special handstamps were in use on the day of issue. Although the wedding day was a public holiday posting boxes were provided at a number of sites for collectors to obtain special handstamps with the much coveted 29 July date. In addition mail posted in special boxes at most main post offices between 23-28 July was cancelled with ordinary operational handstamps dated 29 July. 1981 has also seen celebrations marking the 25th anniversary of the Duke of Edinburgh's Award Scheme and the Post Office commemorated the anniversary with a set of four stamps on 12 August and 12 special handstamps were used on that date.

Apart from these two major events, handstamps have been used on a number of occasions to mark royal visits, the first of these on 11 April to commemorate the Queen Mother's visit to Cornwall where she opened a new hospital in Truro *(Fig. 1).* Approximately 4000 covers were cancelled with this handstamp. On 9 May the Queen opened the new oil terminal at Sullom Voe, Shetland. The day was partly marred by an explosion but happily this did not affect the royal visit. A special handstamp was used at Lerwick H.P.O. — 2903 covers were posted to receive it *(Fig. 2).* A few days later the Queen opened the new Wood Green Shopping City in north London (13 May). The handstamp *(Fig. 3)* was applied to 4543 covers. The handstamp marking the royal visit to South Woodham Ferrers (21 May) was stamped on 4982 pieces of mail *(Fig. 4).* The Queen visited the English National Opera on 28 May; surprisingly only 1323 items of mail were stamped with the attractive handstamp *(Fig. 5).* The Queen and Prince Philip visited Cambridge the following day to open the University's new Edinburgh Building; the Duke is Chancellor of the University. The handstamp *(Fig. 6)* was applied to 4825 covers. Meanwhile Prince Charles was travelling in the North and Midlands — on 29 May he visited Blackpool *(Fig. 7)* and on 2/3 June was at Worcester where three different handstamps were used — one to commemorate his visit to the city, one to mark his unveiling of a statue of Elgar *(Fig. 8)* and one for his visit to the Worcester College for the Blind. He also visited Stoke-on-Trent

on 3 June *(Fig. 9,* 5360 posted). A week later (10 June) he opened the new Post Office building in Bradford *(Fig. 10,* approx. 2200 posted) where he was presented with a framed set of the forthcoming Royal Wedding stamps by the Chairman-designate of the Post Office Mr Ron Dearing. Meanwhile his mother visited Bassetlaw (Nottinghamshire) on 5 June *(Fig. 11,* 1720 posted) opened the National Westminster Bank Tower (11 June — *handstamp not illustrated)* and on 13 June took the salute at the annual Trooping the Colour ceremony in London where a much reported and alarming incident took place involving a youth with a replica gun. Two handstamps were used — one by the British Forces Postal Service (posting box at Inglis Barracks, Mill Hill) and one at the South Western District Office (posting box at Central Hall, Westminster) *(Figs. 12 & 13).* At the beginning of July the Queen visited the Royal Show at Kenilworth *(Fig. 14,* 1965 posted) before moving on to Edinburgh for the Royal Review *(Fig. 15,* 1019 posted). On 17 July she opened the impressive new Humber Bridge. Three different handstamps were used for this event *(Figs. 16-18).*

The Royal Wedding

The Post Office provided three handstamps for the first day of issue of the Wedding stamps — at the Philatelic Bureau, Edinburgh, at the London Chief Office (near St Paul's) and at Caernarfon — scene of the Prince's investiture in July 1969 *(Figs. 19-21).* Numbers of covers posted at the Bureau and L.C.O. are not yet known; the Caernarfon Post Office dealt with 128,496 items of mail. A further 17 sponsored handstamps were in use — possibly the most attractive of which was used at Caernarfon depicting a full view of the medieval castle. The special posting box was situated at the Gift Shop within the castle *(Fig. 22,* 19,498 posted). Special posting facilities were also available at other places having a direct connexion with the wedding and its principal characters. A delightful view of the west front of the Cathedral was incorporated in a handstamp used on mail posted in a box at the Cathedral Stamps shop in the St Paul's Shopping Precinct *(Fig. 23)* and a large cancel including in the design the Cathedral steps and dome, the Prince of Wales's feathers and the arms of St Paul's was in use on mail posted in a box at the Cathedral from 22 July to 21 August *(Fig. 24).* (This cancel was available with the 29 July date and is obviously the key handstamp in the collection.) A posting box was provided in the tea rooms at Althorp House, the home of the bride's father Earl Spencer. The handstamp depicted the impressive frontage of

the House; over 30,000 items of mail received this cancellation *(Fig. 25)*. A charming design in the shape of a parchment reminds us that the first Prince of Wales was proclaimed at Lincoln in 1301 *(Fig. 26, 3550 posted)*. This first prince — later King Edward II — was granted extensive lands in Wales by his father Edward I and the title Prince of Wales was generally used. The title, however, was not actually granted by charter until later. In 1947 the wedding dress for Princess Elizabeth (now the Queen) was made of silk produced at the Lullingstone Silk Farm near Eynsford in Kent. This silk farm — the last operating in England — is now situated at Compton House near Sherborne, Dorset and silk spun there was used to make the stunning dress worn by Lady Diana. The Farm expressed its loyal greetings in the handstamp shown at *Fig. 27* — 10,435 covers were posted. The other handstamps in use on 22 July do not have such direct connexions with the bride and groom but are nevertheless of interest. These are illustrated — *Figs. 28-37*. Numbers posted (where known) were: East of England Show — 4734; Todd Scales — 4494; Chingford Church — 4000; Exeter Stamp Exhibition — 16,537; Canoe Championships — 4348; Canterbury — approx. 22,000.

The Post Office in association with Lever Brothers Ltd are offering a free souvenir cover bearing the Wedding stamps to customers sending proof of purchase of Lever products to their factory at Port Sunlight. The stamps on these covers are cancelled with a non-pictorial handstamp *(Fig. 38)*. This cancellation is also available by the usual reposting facility, covers should be sent to the H.P.O. at Liverpool. The handstamp was introduced on 22 July and remains in use until 31 December. *(A similar souvenir cover offer was made last year in connexion with the Railway stamps — over 500,000 covers were sent out and it is likely that the Royal Wedding covers will prove even more popular.)*

On the night before the wedding, Prince Charles accompanied by his parents, other members of the Royal Family and many foreign heads of state and government attended a spectacular fireworks display in Hyde Park. A special cancellation was used although no posting box was actually provided in the Park. Mail to receive the cancellation had to be sent to the S.W.D.O. *(Fig. 39)*. Also on 28 July a special handstamp depicting St Paul's Cathedral was used on mail posted at the Philatex exhibition in Bournemouth *(Fig. 40 — approx. 2800 posted)*.

On the Wedding day itself postmarks were provided at three places having a direct connexion with the Royal Family. *Solution*, Paternoster Square, near the Cathedral, sponsored the 'Bride and Groom' cancel *(Fig. 41)* and mail posted in a box at Tetbury — near the Prince's new home Highgrove House — received a rectangular cancellation *(Fig. 42, 18,836 posted)*. Lincoln — where the first Prince of Wales was proclaimed — provided the third such cancellation *(Fig. 43 — 3200 posted)*. Other cancellations were provided at Leicester *(Fig. 44)*, Swansea *(not illustrated, of similar design to Leicester, approx. 2800 posted)*, B.F.P.S. 1783 (Inglis Barracks) *(Fig. 45)*, Southport (Box at Prince of Wales Hotel) *(Fig. 46)*, Wootton Bassett *(Fig. 47)*, Arundel *(Fig. 48, 12,154 posted)* and the British Library *(Fig. 49)*. To advertise the Royal Wedding crown produced by the Pobjoy Mint Ltd of Sutton, Surrey for the Isle of Man government, a slogan cancellation was used at Sutton from 22 June to 1 August *(Fig. 50)*.

Duke of Edinburgh Award Scheme

The 25th Anniversary of the Duke of Edinburgh Award Scheme stamps were issued on 12 August and 12 handstamps were used on that date. Two were provided by the Post Office — at the Philatelic Bureau, Edinburgh and at the Paddington D.O. London W2 *(Figs. 51 & 52)*. Over 170,000 covers received the Edinburgh cancellation; 50,020 the Paddington handstamp. Souvenir covers were produced for the Award Scheme by Cotswold Covers of Chippenham, Wilts., and five special handstamps were sponsored for use on these covers. A box was provided at the Queen's Gallery, Buckingham Palace and a handstamp depicting the Scheme's logo was applied to mail posted there *(Fig. 53)*.

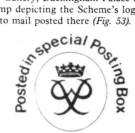

Other boxes were provided at the Palace of Holyroodhouse, Edinburgh and Cardiff Castle *(Figs. 54 & 55)*. A box for the Mansion House cancel was provided at the Post Office, 10 Lombard Street, London EC3 and for the Belfast postmark at the Hillsborough Post Office, Co. Down *(Figs. 56 & 57)*. Special cachets were applied to covers ordered from the official agents although the posting boxes for the Hillsborough Castle and Mansion House cancels were not provided at those sites according to the Post Office's *Postmark Bulletin (Fig. 58* shown above).

Other cancels used on 12 August are shown in *Figs. 59-63*. Numbers posted (where known) were: Hull — 5000; Leicester → 8908; Winchmore Hill — 9315. A slogan advertising the Duke of Edinburgh Award crowns produced for the Manx government was used at Sutton, Surrey from 3 August to 26 September *(Fig. 64)*. A special Royal Wedding Decorated Tram cancel was applied to mail posted at the Crich Tramway Museum near Matlock on 29 August *(Fig 65 — 4674 posted)*.

At the time of writing the Post Office have just announced that special handstamps will be used at Cardiff and Caernarfon on 27 October to celebrate the visit to the Principality of Prince Charles and his wife. This will be the first visit to Wales by the new Princess. A special handstamp will also be used at Newcastle on 6 November when the Queen opens the new Metro railway. These will be illustrated here later.

Few of these cancellations will ever be worth much in monetary terms but collectors who have obtained specimens — especially those who have obtained a complete collection — will have interesting and nostalgic souvenirs of a memorable Royal Year. In their own humble way the many Royal Wedding postmarks will recall those few hours on 29 July when the World's troubles were forgotten and the nation indulged — as the Archbishop of Canterbury told us — in '. . . the stuff of which fairy-tales are made'.

The writer acknowledges the assistance of the staffs of many Post Offices in providing information about the numbers of covers posted to receive special handstamps. The illustrations of the cachets used on 12 August are by courtesy of Cotswold Covers.
(Illustrations reduced to ⅔ size).

ROYAL WEDDINGS PAST...

Royal betrothals and weddings are few and far between — few enough, at least, to justify the nation 'letting its hair down' in celebration of the forthcoming marriage of Prince Charles, eldest son of Her Majesty the Queen and the Duke of Edinburgh, to Lady Diana Spencer, daughter of the Earl Spencer and the Hon. Mrs Shand Kydd. Not so long ago — in 1973 — we similarly celebrated the wedding of Princess Anne and Captain Mark Phillips, and then, as now, there were numerous manufactured souvenirs of the joyous event, including commemorative stamps from more than 20 Commonwealth territories as well as Britain, Guernsey, Jersey and the Isle of Man. Again, stamps were issued for the silver weddings of King George VI and Queen Elizabeth, now the Queen Mother (in 1948), and of Queen Elizabeth II and the Duke of Edinburgh (in 1972).

Nine European countries are currently ruled by 'crowned heads', including two Queens, many of them related to our own Royal Family or to dynasties in other countries, and stamps provide a pictorial record of their accessions and marriages, also of those whose reigns were overtaken and terminated by political events.

Baudouin I, King of the Belgians, the elder son of Leopold III and his first wife, the former Princess Astrid of Sweden, married the Spanish Dona Fabiola de Mora y Aragon, daughter of the Conde de Mora and Marqués de Casa Riera, on 15 December 1960 — the event was commemorated by portrait stamps (S.G.1765/7). King Baudouin's sister, Princess Joséphine-Charlotte, married Prince Jean (son of the Grand Duchess Charlotte and Prince Felix of Bourbon-Parma), now the reigning Grand Duke of Luxembourg, on 9 April 1953. Luxembourg issued wedding stamps with portraits of the Royal couple from photographs by E. Kutter (S.G.563/8). Since that time there have been numerous stamp pictures of them and their children — the Princesses Marie Astrid and Margareta, and the Princes Henri (heir-apparent), Jean and Guillaume. The silver wedding of Grand Duke Jean and Grand Duchess Joséphine-Charlotte in 1978 was commemorated by a miniature sheet containing two stamps with contemporary portraits of the couple from a photograph attributed to N. Ketter (S.G.MS1002).

Belgian stamps for the 150th anniversary of the country's independence, issued in 1980 (S.G.2597/MS2602) showed portraits of the reigning Kings and Queens from 1831 — Leopold I and Louise-Marie, Leopold II and Marie-Henrietta, Albert I and Elisabeth, Leopold III and Astrid, and Baudouin and Fabiola.

Ex-Queen Juliana of the Netherlands

married Prince Bernhard of Lippe-Biesterfeld on 7 January 1937. There were no special stamps on this occasion, but there were two for their silver wedding in January 1962 (S.G.919/20), while a striking portrait of Juliana commemorating her 70th birthday was issued in March 1979 (S.G.1310). Following her abdication in 1980, her eldest daughter, Beatrix Wilhelmina Armgard, was installed as Queen on 30 April. Born in 1938, Beatrix married the German diplomat, Prince Claus von Amsberg, on 10 March 1966, and, while

again there were no Dutch stamps to mark the event, the Netherlands Antilles issued a single 25 c. stamp picturing love birds perching on monogrammed wedding rings (S.G.476). They have three sons — Prince Willem-Alexander, Prince Johan Friso and Prince Constantijn. Queen Beatrix has since appeared on stamps issued by the Netherlands and the Netherlands Antilles.

Liechtenstein, the tiny Principality sandwiched between Switzerland and Austria, issued stamps both for the marriage (on 7 March 1943, S.G.214/6) and the silver wedding (1968, S.G.491) of the reigning Prince, Francis Joseph II, and Countess Gina von Wilczek. The wedding stamps showed formal portraits, while the 'silver' stamp depicted the arms of Liechtenstein and Wilczek. There were four sons — and one daughter — of the marriage, and the Crown Prince Hans Adam, heir apparent, was himself married to the Countess Marie Kinsky on 30 July 1967. Their portraits were depicted on two special stamps, issued in a miniature sheet (S.G.MS471).

King Juan Carlos I of Borbon y Borbon acceded to the Spanish throne in November 1975. Born in 1938, the eldest son of Don Juan, Conde de Barcelona, Juan Carlos married, in 1962, Princess Sophie of Greece, daughter of the late King Paul of the Hellenes and the late Queen Frederika. Both are portrayed on the stamps issued by Spain in 1975 to commemorate the proclamation of Spain's first King since Alfonso XIII was deposed on the establishment of the second republic in 1931 (S.G.2347/50).

A glamorous, 'story-book' wedding took place in Monaco on 19 April 1956 when the reigning Prince, Rainier III, married the American film actress, Grace Kelly. Prince Rainier succeeded his grandfather, Louis II, who died in 1949. The eight wedding stamps comprised formal portraits of the Prince and his bride, flanking the crown and their personal monograms — virtually the same design (with discreetly updated portraits) was employed for the five silver wedding stamps issued in May this year (S.G.578/85 and S.G.1467/71). There were three children — Princess Caroline (married, and since divorced), Prince Albert (heir apparent, whose 21st birthday was commemorated by the issue of a miniature sheet in April 1979, (S.G.MS1375), and Princess Stephanie.

Denmark's Queen, Margrethe II, succeeded to the throne following the death of her father, King Frederick IX, in 1972. She married Henri, Count de Monpezat (Prince Henrik of Denmark), on 10 June 1967, an occasion on which both Denmark (S.G.487) and Greenland (S.G.64) issued stamps in a uniform design showing the couple's profiles

in silhouette. The silver wedding of King
Frederick and Queen Ingrid (daughter of the
late King Gustav VI Adolf of Sweden by his
first wife) in 1960 was commemorated by two
stamps (S.G.424/5) showing their full-face
portraits. One of Margrethe's sisters, Princess
Anne-Marie, married Constantine II of Greece
in September 1964, six months since he had
succeeded to the throne after the death of his
father, Paul I, a first cousin of Philip, Duke
of Edinburgh. Paul married the Princess
Frederika Louise, daughter of the Duke of
Brunswick, in 1938 — three stamps marking
the event showed formal portraits of Prince
Paul and his bride (S.G.517/9), while again
the Greek Post Office issued three attractive
stamps in 1964 for Constantine's marriage to
Anne-Marie (S.G.962/4). Following a
revolutionary coup and abortive counter-coup,
King Constantine was forced into exile in
December 1967.

King Haakon VII and Queen Maud (sister
of King George V) of Norway were first
pictured together on two stamps issued for his
golden jubilee in 1955 (S.G.458/9). Their only
child, Olav, born in 1903, married Princess
Martha of Sweden in 1929 and succeeded his
father to the Norwegian throne in 1957.
Stamps commemorating King Olav V's 70th
(S.G.702/3) and 75th (S.G.797/8) birthdays
were issued in 1973 and 1978 respectively.

Carl XVI Gustav, born 1946, succeeded to
the Swedish throne on the death of his
grandfather, Gustav VI Adolf, on 15
September 1973, and he was Europe's most
eligible bachelor until he married Silvia
Renate Sommerlath on 19 June 1976. Both
were pictured on the two Royal Wedding
stamps issued on their wedding day
(S.G.896/7). They have a daughter, Princess
Victoria, who is four this month and who, by
special decree of the Riksdag, became heiress-
apparent to the throne, taking precedence
over her younger brother, Prince Carl. The
new order of succession was the occasion for
two stamps (S.G.1035/6), showing the King
and his pretty daughter, issued in February
1980.

, Three Italian stamps (S.G.267/9) — and
three from Cyrenaica (Libya: S.G.58/60) —
commemorated the marriage of Crown Prince
Umberto, son of King Victor Emmanuel III
of Italy, to Princess Marie-José of Belgium
(King Baudouin's aunt) in 1930. Following
Victor Emmanuel's abdication in 1946,
Umberto reigned briefly for a few weeks until
13 June when he left the country after
demonstrations in favour of a republic. King
Zog I of Albania was similarly forced into
exile in 1939, when the Italians occupied his
country — eight stamps and a miniature sheet
were issued for his marriage to the Countess
Geraldine Apponyi of Hungary in 1938
(S.G.321/MS328a). King Boris III of Bulgaria
married Princess Giovanna of Savoy in 1930
and there were special stamps to mark the
event (S.G.300/3). Boris died suddenly while
on a visit to Germany in 1943.

From Egypt we have reminders of
romantic alliances of the distant past — that
of the beautiful Nefertiti, wife of King
Akhnaton (Amenhetep IV) of the 14th century
B.C., whose famous scuptured head,
discovered at Amarna, is featured on several

Egyptian stamps, and also that of the almost legendary Cleopatra, Queen of Egypt (S.G.74), who first captivated Caesar, then Mark Antony, and, following the latter's suicide, poisoned herself with an asp in 30 B.C. In more recent times, King Farouk and his bride, Farida, were depicted on an Egyptian stamp (S.G.265) issued for their wedding in January 1938 — a similar stamp issued a few weeks later for Farouk's 18th birthday (S.G.272) showed Farida in her wedding dress. In 1951 another wedding stamp recorded Farouk's second marriage — to Narriman Sadek (S.G.367 and a miniature sheet, MS368). Her role as Queen was all too brief for in 1952 there was a *coup d'etat* and Farouk was forced to abdicate and go into exile.

The late Mohammed Riza Pahlevi, Shah of Persia, married Farouk's sister, Princess Fawzia, in 1939 (S.G.831/5) — eventually the marriage was annulled and, in 1951, the Shah married Soraya Esfandiari (S.G.959/64) whom he also later divorced, both wives having failed to produce a male heir. Third time lucky — in December 1959, the Shah married Farah Diba, daughter of an army officer, the event being commemorated by two wedding stamps in September 1960 (S.G.1220/1), and the long-awaited birth of a Crown Prince — Riza Pahlavi — in October 1960 was also celebrated by two stamps showing the family group in 1961. Following widespread unrest, the Shah and his family left Iran in January 1979, and in April Iran was declared an Islamic Republic by Ayatollah Khomeini, principal leader of the Shi'ah Moslems.

King Hussein of Jordan married Princess Dina in 1955 (S.G.443/4), divorced in 1957, and in 1961 he married an English girl, Toni Gardiner ('Princess Muna'), divorced in 1972 — no stamps were issued. His third marriage, to Alia Toukan, was sadly terminated in 1977 when she died in an air crash — stamps issued in that year depicted the Royal couple (S.G.1222/5), and Queen Alia as the subject of a special commemorative issue (S.G.1226/9). There were three stamps in 1969 for the wedding of Crown Prince Hassan (1968), younger brother of the King, pictured with his bride (S.G.850/2).

Weddings and anniversaries have been a recurring feature of Japanese stamps — first Emperor Mutsuhito's silver wedding, 1894 (S.G.126/7); the wedding of the Imperial Prince Yoshihito and Prince Sadako in 1900 (S.G.152) — he was Emperor of Japan from 1912 to 1926 — and their silver wedding, 1925 (S.G.226/9); and Crown Prince Akihito's marriage to Princess Michiko in 1959 (S.G.798/MS802). Two stamps issued in 1974 commemorated the golden wedding of Emperor Hirohito (S.G.1339/MS1341) who married Princess Nagako in 1924, and succeeded his father, Yoshihito, on the throne in 1926. Nepal commemorated the wedding of Crown Prince (now King) Birendra and Princess Aishwarya with a single stamp (S.G.247) in 1970, while King Bhumibol of Thailand married Princess Sirikit in April 1950 — just a week before he was crowned. Two 15th wedding anniversary stamps were issued in 1965 (S.G.521/2) and two silver wedding stamps in 1975 (S.G.833/4).

...ROYAL WEDDING PRESENT

When Prince Charles reached the mature age of 30 years on 14 November 1978, it became increasingly apparent that the heir to the throne could — or would — not much longer delay his choice of bride and marriage plans. From that time speculation was rife and there was hardly a national newspaper which did not, at one time or another, link his name with one or other of his numerous female acquaintances. Thus the announcement of his betrothal to Lady Diana Spencer (on 24 February this year) was welcomed by the British people and Press, while the Post Office and Commonwealth postal administrations were able to 'dust off' their contingency plans for special stamps and set the wheels of design and production in motion. That such plans existed is evident by the alacrity with which the stamps were announced and described — and five months is just long enough for them to be designed and printed.

The two GB stamps — 14p and 25p — will picture the Royal couple based on an engagement photograph, in vertical format, and they are due for issue on Wednesday 22 July, a week before the marriage ceremony in St Paul's Cathedral. The Crown Agents are launching an elaborate omnibus series of issues for the territories they represent — 22 of them from Ascension to Western Samoa. Each country is issuing three stamps — the low-value stamp depicts a traditional English wedding bouquet consisting of the flowers of the issuing country; the middle value shows Prince Charles as a 'man of action', a different scene for each country and, in some instances, showing the Prince during a visit to that country. The third stamp (top value) depicts Prince Charles and Lady Diana from one of the official 'engagement day' photographs, unchanged throughout the series.

The stamp borders, in the form of an oval garland, are composed of the heraldic devices on the Order of the Garter as worn by Prince Charles, and from the coat-of arms of Lady Diana Spencer, surmounted by the Prince of Wales' ostrich feathers, which are thought to have been inherited from Philippa of Hainault, wife of Edward III. The feathers also bear the Prince's motto, 'Ich Dien', which, translated from the German, means 'I Serve'. The designers were J. C. G. George and Peter Spurrier, Pursuivants of the College of Arms.

On the middle values, Prince Charles will be seen in various military uniforms — as Colonel-in-Chief of the Cheshire Regiment, the Royal Regiment of Wales and of the Gordon Highlanders, also as a Colonel of the Welsh Guards, and as a naval flyer and a helicopter pilot. His sporting activities are

well represented — polo, riding, skiing, sailing and cross-country events, while formal events such as his Investiture as Prince of Wales are in contrast to the informal portraits and visits abroad. The Hong Kong $1.30 stamp shows him 'dotting the eye' of a ceremonial dragon during his visit there. Prince Charles joined the Royal Navy in September 1971 and progressed from Dartmouth to take command of his own ship, the 360-ton mine-hunter, HMS *Bronington*, in the ensuing five years. He has a natural aptitude for flying and first flew solo in 1969: in 1971 he entered the RAF (in which he holds the rank of Wing Commander) and he started flying helicopters in 1974. The Prince is a skilful and dedicated polo player, though not quite so successful 'jumping the sticks' — he has had one or two falls.

Guernsey, Jersey and the Isle of Man are issuing stamps for the Royal Wedding. Seven Guernsey stamps (8p and 12p in *se-tenant* strips of three plus a single 25p) and a miniature sheet will be released on 29 July; Jersey's two stamps, 10p and 25p, on the 28th. The two Manx stamps, 9p and 25p, and a miniature sheet containing two sets, are also due on 29 July. Australia has planned two stamps, 22 c. and 60 c., and the Cocos (Keeling) Islands, 24 c. and 60 c., for issue on the 29th. Gibraltar will issue a £1 stamp featuring the Royal couple on 27 July, while Cyprus will issue a 200 m. stamp as part of the Anniversary/Events issue of September or October. Kenya is planning to release five stamps depicting Prince Charles on safari and with the late President Jomo Kenyatta and his wife, Ngina, when he and Princess Anne visited Kenya in February 1971; the Royal Yacht *Britannia;* St Paul's Cathedral; and a picture of the Royal couple in a souvenir sheet.

The Royal Yacht *Britannia*, designed by Sir Victor Shepheard, KCB, was built in 1953 at John Brown's shipyard on Clydebank. Described as a floating royal palace, she has a capacious royal suite and the facilities to receive and entertain guests. The *Britannia* is listed as a vessel of Her Majesty's Fleet and classified as 'Royal Yacht/Hospital Ship' (in time of war). She has travelled the world extensively on numerous royal tours and visits abroad.

The designs and artwork for the Crown Agents' omnibus issue were prepared by John Waddington's Studio of Leeds, who also printed some of the stamps, sharing this task with The House of Questa, Harrison & Sons, Format International Security Printers, and Walsall Security Printers. All the stamps were printed in lithography except those of Hong Kong which were printed (by Harrison & Sons) in photogravure.

The John Waddington Studio also designed the Royal Wedding stamps commissioned by the Inter-Governmental Philatelic Corporation of New York for Antigua, Ghana, Commonwealth of Dominica, Grenada and Grenadines of Grenada, Maldives Republic, Turks & Caicos Islands, Uganda, St Lucia, and also Bhutan and Cameroun. The stamps show the engaged couple, the Royal residences such as Balmoral and Sandringham, Prince Charles and the Royal Yacht *Britannia*, ceremonial coaches and a helicopter of the Queen's Flight.

Independent Anguilla has four attractive Wedding stamps picturing the Prince and his fiancée with background pictures of Althorp, Northamptonshire, the magnificent 16th-century ancestral home of the Spencers (Lady Diana's parents), St Paul's Cathedral, Windsor Castle and Buckingham Palace.

Last (but not least!) comes a formidable omnibus series of Royal Wedding stamps sponsored by Philatelists (1980) Ltd of Bristol, representing Kiribati, Montserrat, Nevis, St Kitts, St Vincent, St Vincent Grenadines and Tuvalu. Each country is issuing sets of three sheetlets, each containing six identical stamps plus one double-size, 'greetings' stamp portraying the Royal couple. The designs, by Derek Shults, feature royal yachts from the mid-17th century, with the Royal Yacht *Britannia* featured on the top-value sheetlet of each country. Details —

Country	Denominations	Total Face Value of Sheetlets
Kiribati	12 c., 50 c., $2	$17.64
Montserrat	90 c., $3, $4	$55.30
Nevis	55 c., $2, $5	$52.85
St Kitts	55 c., $2.50, $4	$49.35
St Vincent	60 c., $2.50, $4	$49.70
St Vincent Grenadines	50 c., $3, $3.50	$49.00
Tuvalu	10 c., 45 c., $2	$17.85

Issue dates were announced as 'June/July'.

Summary of Crown Agents' omnibus issues

Ascension Island	— 10p, 15p, 50p
Barbados	— 28 c., 50 c., $2.50
Bermuda	— 30 c., 50 c., $1
British Virgin Islands	— 10 c., 35 c., $1.25
Brunei	— 10 sen, $1, $2
Cayman Islands	— 20 c., 30 c., $1
Falkland Islands	— 10p. 13p. 52p
Falkland Islands Dependencies	— 10p., 13p, 52p
Fiji	— 6 c., 45 c., $1
The Gambia	— 75 b, D 1, D 1.25
Hong Kong	— 20 c., $1.30, $5
Lesotho	— 25s., 50s. 75s.
Mauritius	— 25 c., Rs. 2.50, Rs. 10
Norfolk Island	— 35 c., 55 c., 60 c.
Pitcairn Islands	— 20 c., 35 c., $1.20
St Helena	— 14p, 29p, 32p
Sierra Leone	— 31 c., 45 c., Le 1
Solomon Islands	— 8 c., 45 c., $1
Swaziland	— 10 c., 25 c., E 1
Tristan da Cunha	— 5p, 20p, 50p
Vanuatu	— 15 vatus, 45 vatus, 75 vatus
Western Samoa	— 18 sene, 32 sene, $1

These issues will be released on 22 July, with the exception of Brunei and Hong Kong (29 July) and Swaziland (21 July).

Did you miss the boat or did you take our advice?

In 1973 we recommended and sold the British definitive 1/2p (SGX842) with one phosphor band on side. We told our customers to buy them at 25p each. WE WERE RIGHT!! Today this stamp is catalogued at £55.00 each. If you had taken our advice, for an outlay of only £50 in1973, the current catalogue value of your investment would be a staggering total of £11,000.00.

In 1999 we recommended our customers to buy the Princess Diana Welsh Language Presentation Packs. The catalogue value was only £2.50 each, but we were telling our customers to buy them for up to double catalogue value £5 each. Within only 6 years they had increased by 5,900%.

As everyone knows, investments can go down as well as up and the past in not necessarily a guide to the future. However, being selective and taking sound advice is the best way to make your hobby pay for itself.

In 2003 we recommended our customers to buy the Coronation £1 Green (SG 2380) which was catalogued by Stanley Gibbons at £1.50 per stamp. Within 1 year the catalogue value had increased to £50 per stamp, an increase of over 3,200%. In 2004 we told our customers to buy the Fruit & Veg Presentation Pack – it was catalogued at £4.50. We said ignore the catalogue value, it's cheap at even treble the catalogue value – this pack increased in

Stanley Gibbons Catalogue to £60 within two years; an increase of well over 1,200%. We hope that you took our advice in 2004. We recommended you to buy the Locomotives Miniature Sheet (SG.MS.2423). The Stanley Gibbons Catalogue value was £3.75 each. Within 1 year the Stanley Gibbons Catalogue had increased to £25 each - An increase of over 550% in only one year.

In 2005 we recommended the 2003 Rugby Presentation Pack. The 2005 Stanley Gibbons concise catalogue listed this at £6 and, within 3 years, the catalogue value had soared. The 2008 Concise Catalogue value for the Rugby Presentation Pack was £35 each, a truly massive increase. We hope you took our advice.

In 2008 we recommended the 2002 Bridges of London Presentation pack (number 338). At the time the catalogue value was £8 each. Within 1 year of our recommendation the catalogue value of the Presentation Pack increased to £25 each. This year the catalogue value increased once again from £25 per pack to £55 per pack.

Earlier this year we recommended our customers to buy the Nobel Prizes Presentation Pack, the SG catalogue value was £10 each. In the latest SG catalogue the price zoomed to a staggering £50 each. Our customers have complimented us and said once again "You were right!"

PLEASE LISTEN TO US NOW!

We now strongly recommend you to buy the Great Britain 2001 Flags Presentation packs No. MO6, at the best possible price.

For our most recent up to the minute recommendations Please telephone 01273 326994

12 Prince Albert Street, Brighton, Sussex BN1 1HE
Tel: 01273 326994

STAMP PORTRAITS OF QUEEN ELIZABETH II from the photographs of Anthony Buckley

Lois E. Young

When Queen Elizabeth came to the throne in 1953, Dorothy Wilding's Royal Portraits which had dominated the latter part of her father's reign, still held pride of place. But as we moved into the 1960's Anthony Buckley's work began to take over in the stamp scene.

Various poses are photographed at one sitting, and by studying the hair-style, dress and jewellery, it is possible to identify those taken at one time, and so to place them in groups.

In the following classification it seems likely that Groups 2 and 3, also 4 and 5 were not separate sittings, as the only difference between the two, in each case, is the removal of the tiara.

GROUP 1. The hair is combed up in front, curled on nape of neck and above the ear, which is covered to lobe, crown of head smooth.

The dress has jewelled embroidery from the bust downwards, neckline curved to centre 'v' and shoulder-straps. The Garter Sash is worn over the left shoulder. Jewellery. The diamond fringe tiara, which formerly belonged to Queen Alexandra, three row diamond necklace, cluster earrings, bracelet on each wrist, Garter Star and the Family Honours (painted miniatures of King George V and King George VI).

The poses used are: 1A. Face in profile looking left, shoulders turned slightly to left. 1B. Face in profile looking left, but with right eye showing more, and with

Group 1

TRISTAN DA CUNHA 10/- 10/-

ADA 5
POSTAGE

shoulders turned more to the left than in 1A. 1C. Face nearly full, right arm a little forward.

Examples: 1A. ¾ length versions on Canada T240, Papua & New Guinea T37 and Niue T35. Cook I. T52 is shoulder length and the head is used on Turks & Caicos T101 and as small inset on many stamps, e.g. Turks & Caicos T85 and Cook I. T76 (Victor Whiteley's cameo head.) 1B. Tristan T44 (shoulder length), Antigua T54 (head, showing necklace), Mauritius T86 (head). 1C. Grenada T65 (¾ length), Bermuda T87 (head).

GROUP 2. The hair style is similar to Group 1. The dress of figured material has sleeves and a square neck. The Queen wears the diamond scroll tiara with diamond points, given her as a wedding present by Queen Mary. The diamond necklace is of round stones separated by links, and she has diamond stud earrings.
The poses used are: 2A. Shoulders and face turned slightly to left. 2B. ¾ face looking left. 2C. Profile looking left. 2D. Full face. 2E. Face turned slightly to right. 2F. ¾ face looking right.
Examples: 2A. Dominica T79 (head and shoulders), St Vincent T32 (head). 2B. Pitcairn T35, Australia T160. 2C. Virgin T58. 2D. Profile looking left. 2E. Gilbert & Ellice T22. 2E. St Kitts T32. 2F. Virgin T59.
Note. 2B. can be distinguished from the Wilding photograph No 015924 0. ¾ face looking left, in which the Queen wears the same tiara, by the fact that in the Wilding portrait half of the ear is visible, but in the Buckley 2B the hair covers all save the lobe.

GROUP 3. Hair, dress and jewellery the same as Group 2 but without tiara.
The poses are: 3A. Full face. 3B. Face turned slightly to left. 3C. Profile facing left.
Examples: The only use of 3A. is with a portrait of Prince Philip, on Mauritius T142. 3B. Fiji T79. 3C. Australia T161.

GROUP 4. Hair, full above forehead and ears, hides much of the tiara from the front, slight dip on crown of head, half of ear visible.
Dress has all-over jewelled embroidery, oval neckline and shoulder straps. The Garter Sash, with the Family Honours is over the Queen's left shoulder. She wears the diamond scroll tiara (as in Group 2.), a necklace of even-sized diamonds with round pendant and matching pendant earrings.

Poses are: 4A. Face looking slightly to right, shoulders facing front. 4B. Profile looking right, shoulders facing front. 4C. Face and shoulders turned to left, right eye just suggested. 4D. Profile looking left.
Examples: 4A. Mauritius Royal Visit 1972 2r. 50. S.G. 456. 4B. St Helena T72. 4C. New Zealand T263, Virgin T63. 4D. Pitcairn T45, Bahamas T82. Note. Bahamas T81 bears a profile facing right, but the position of the Garter Sash over the right shoulder instead of left, shows this to be a reversed printing of 4D rather than a fresh pose. I also think Grenada T170 is probably a reversed printing of 4C. Photogravure and lithogravure reversed or 'mirror-image' printings are more of a problem in the Buckley portraits than they are in the Wilding's where the hair parting is a vital clue.

GROUP 5. Hair, dress and jewellery as Group 4 but without tiara.
Poses are: 5A. ¾ Face looking left. 5B. Face turned a little more to front than 5A, more hair by right eye. 5C. Profile facing left. Note. 5C can be distinguished from 3C by the drop earrings worn in Groups 4 and 5 as opposed to the round stud earrings in Groups 2 and 3.
Examples: 5A. Canada T257, Bermuda T69. 5B. Bermuda T74. 5C. Virgin Is. T64 and 67. Gibraltar T65 4d. and 9d. are reversed 5C.

Two new Anthony Buckley portraits, of each of which we have, as yet, only one pose are:

6. A full face portrait of the Queen, with shoulders turned a little to the right. Dress, sleeveless, with oval neckline and Garter Sash. She wears the pearl and diamond tiara bought by Queen Mary from a Russian Grand Duchess in 1921, a necklace of even sized diamonds with pendant, and matching drop earrings. This portrait was used for the Commonwealth Heads of Government Meeting stamp, 1973 Canada T359.

7. Another full face portrait, with shoulders turned a little to the right, with similar dress and Garter Sash, but wearing the diamond scroll tiara, a necklace of oblong sapphires with an oblong pendant, a matching bracelet and pendant earrings. A ¾ length version appears in the New Zealand Day stamp sheet 1974, T341 and a head and shoulders on the Br Solomons Is Royal Visit 1974 T95.

Type numbers given are from Gibbon's Commonwealth Catalogue.

Group 2

Group 3

Group 4

Group 5

Portrait 6

Portrait 7

A Royal Wedding

HRH Prince William to marry Miss Catherine Middleton

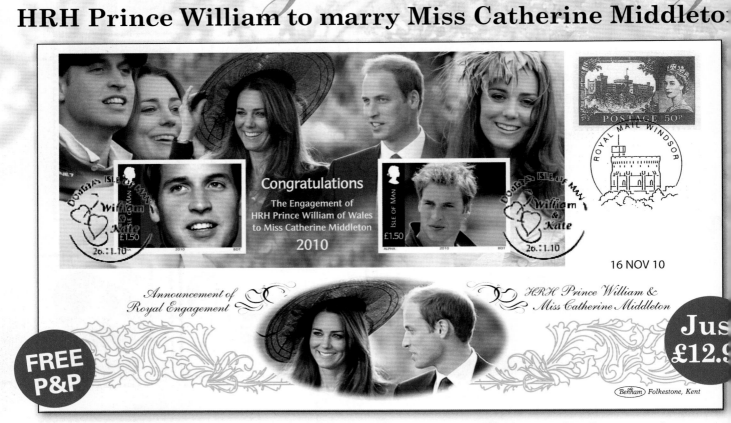

Congratulations
The Engagement of
HRH Prince William of Wales
to Miss Catherine Middleton
2010

Announcement of Royal Engagement

HRH Prince William & Miss Catherine Middleton

16 NOV 10

Benham Folkestone, Kent

FREE P&P

Just £12.9

The engagement of HRH Prince William of Wales, second in line to the throne, and Miss Catherine (Kate) Middleton was announced from Clarence House on 16th November 2010.

The eagerly anticipated news was greeted by a surge of happiness and joy across the nation and indeed around the world.

A special commemorative first day cover marks this momentous occasion.

The envelope bears the delightful Isle of Man stamp sheet with two stamps depicting The Prince and images of the happy couple in the border. It bears a Douglas, Isle of Man postmark on 26th November 2010 - the day the sheet was issued. The cover also bears a Windsor Castle 50p definitive with a 16th November, Windsor postmark - the date the engagement was actually announced.

A beautiful and highly collectable souvenir of a very special day in our nation's history.

Prince William and Kate Middleton Stamp Collection

To commemorate this historic Royal occasion, countries around the world will be producing new stamp issues. Issuing authorites confirmed so far are Jersey, IoM, Micronesia and Gibraltar. and we expect the following countries to also be issuing: British Indian Ocean Territory, British Virgin Islands, Fiji, Jamaica, Kiribati, St. Helena, Tristan Da Cunha, St. Vincent, Falklands, South Georgia, Ascension and the Bahamas.

To be assured of not missing out on any of these exciting issues, why not sign up now and we will ensure you receive these historic issues as and when they are released. This collection will be **limited to just 2011 worldwide**, a very small quantity given the importance of the event. Each sending, which will comprise stamps, sheetlets or miniatur sheets, will be supplied on luxury hingeless pages and priced at just £18.50 per sending.

A free album will also be supplied to house your precious collection and a special frontispiece confirming its limited edition status will be sent with your final instalment.

This will be a stunning collection so do not miss out - sign up today!

Pre-orde now to b assured receivin one of th collectio

Call us on our order hotline: 0844 994 9400 or fill in the order form below

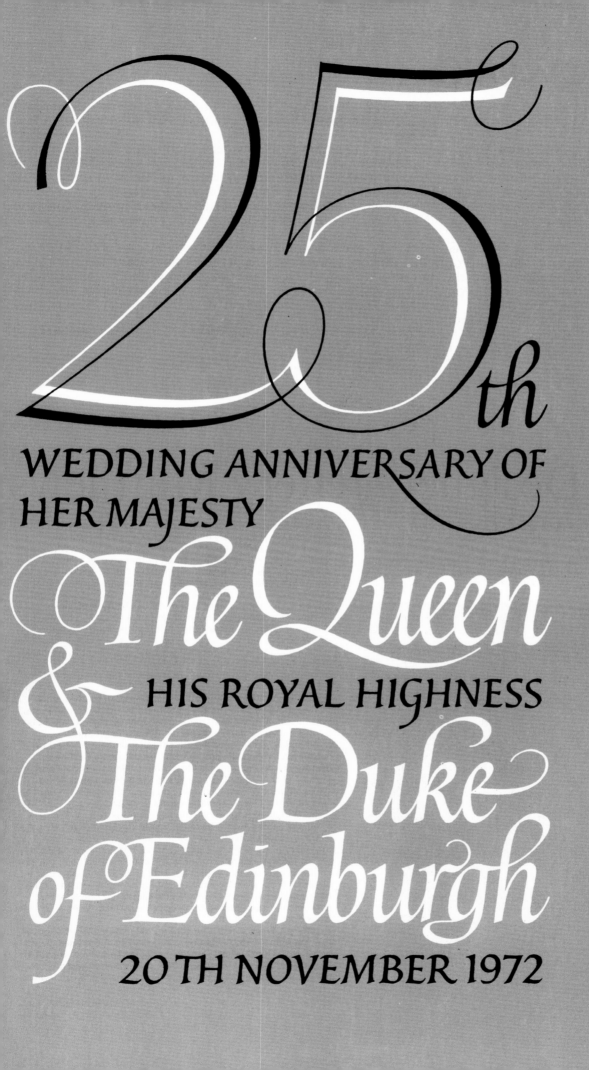

25th

WEDDING ANNIVERSARY OF HER MAJESTY

The Queen

HIS ROYAL HIGHNESS

& The Duke of Edinburgh

20TH NOVEMBER 1972

Foreword

On the 20th of this month—November 1972—the British Post Office will issue two stamps in commemoration of the Silver Wedding of Her Majesty Queen Elizabeth II and His Royal Highness Prince Philip, Duke of Edinburgh.

Of all recent stamp issues, this one is a classic example of the results which come from a properly controlled and co-ordinated design programme. From the initial exploration of possible design solutions, through a number of preliminary design experiments right up to the final essaying of the Stamp Advisory Committee's recommendations to the Palace, the whole project had involved designer, photographer and printer in a carefully directed exercise of design development. Later the same designer was asked to design a First Day Cover and Presentation Pack, as well as promotional material.

In this regard, the Post Office received the closest co-operation from the Palace, for when it was decided to work towards a photographic design, Her Majesty graciously gave permission for new photographs to be taken especially for reproduction, by Norman Parkinson. Without such valuable assistance, Jeffery Matthews would not have had available for his design photographs which he himself supervised, nor would the printers have had origination of the technical quality they demanded for miniature reproduction.

The results of this co-operation are stamps which will be admired by the world and cherished in the albums of stamp collectors everywhere.

The Designer: Jeffery Matthews

Jeffery Matthews, a graphic designer and calligrapher of exceptional ability and reputation, is already well known for his stamp designs for the Post Office. Besides the new Silver Wedding stamps, he also designed the two special postmarks, the first day cover and the presentation pack.

He was born in 1928 in East Dulwich, London, and lived in that area all of his early life. His father, Henry Matthews, Freeman, Citizen and Goldsmith of London, had a workshop in Clerkenwell, and was well known in that area as a master craftsman. The Matthews family history can be traced back to the 16th century, when 'Fine Knives' were made by Richard Matthews on Fleet Bridge circa 1563. The business of 'Gold Watch Case-making' was founded in 1818 by Frederick Matthews, and handed down from father to son. Jeffery's brother, Martin, continues the craft into the fourth generation of the family, and among other work cases rare antique watches.

As a young man, Jeffery helped his father in the workshop during his spare time to earn pocket-money, but despite his inherent skill as a craftsman, his interests and drawing ability led him in other directions. He studied interior decoration and design at the Brixton School of Building with the vague idea of designing sets for the then booming film industry. Lettering was included in the curriculum, and Jeffery became fascinated by this subject and developed his interest in graphics.

When he had finished his training, he worked in a design studio for three years, and in 1952 he became a freelance designer, working with his close friend, Alan Harmer, who had studied at the Royal College of Art. Work was scarce at first and such jobs as were available ranged from sign-writing shop fascias to the design and artwork for book-jackets.

In 1953, when Jeffery married, he and his wife, Chris, took a flat and studio over a baker's shop in Peckham Rye. At Whitsun, the following year, Alan Harmer was tragically drowned in a boating accident, and at first Jeffery thought he would have to return to work in someone else's studio, but he contined to work alone with his wife as secretary and assistant, teaching art at evening classes to augment their income. All his work comes simply by recommendation of one client to another, and through the Design Council's Record of Designers.

Jeffery's first introduction to the Post Office was through this Record in 1959, when he was asked to submit designs for two stamps for the Post Office Charter Tercentenary. Between December 1960 and October 1963, he submitted designs for the Post Office Savings Bank Centenary, the CEPT Conference,

SW 2

National Productivity Year, the Paris Postal Conference and the International Lifeboat Conference.

In 1965, just when he was beginning to feel that he was 'always the bridesmaid, never the blushing bride', he had his first stamps issued—two designs for the United Nations' 20th Anniversary, 3d. and 1s. 6d. In 1967, two of his designs for the British Bridges issue were selected—the 4d. Tarr Steps, and the 1s. 9d. M4 Motorway Viaduct, and he also designed the FDC and presentation pack. His wife, who writes under the name of Charity Boxall, wrote the feature on bridges for the pack. Jeffery was featured as one of the three designers in the Post Office film, 'Picture to Post' (1969).

In May 1968, he designed the first day covers for the new 4d. and 5d. stamps for Guernsey and Jersey (issued in September 1968), and in the same year he submitted designs for the Anniversary stamps (Atlantic Flight, Australia Flight, NATO and ILO), and also for the Investiture of the Prince of Wales. The special lettered design—'British Rural Architecture'—was prepared by Jeffery, and used on the FDC and pack for the issue of the four stamps in February 1970.

His more recent work includes the complete range of the new GB decimal 'TO PAY' stamps, both low and high value types, and the new decimal stamps for the Isle of Man, Northern Ireland, Scotland, and Wales and Monmouthshire, issued in July 1971.

Other design work covers a wide variety of subjects—designs for book-bindings, book-jackets and title-pages; packaging for foods, stationery etc; security printing—cheques and receipts; symbols, trademarks and complete house-styles; hand-lettering for numerous applications, some even in Russian and Polish!

A recent commission from the Master Baker was the design of a Silver Loving Cup for presentation to the Worshipful Company of Bakers. Jeffery particularly enjoyed this as it was a link with his family's craft.

Jeffery and Chris now live in Beckenham, Kent, with their two children, Rory, 16, and Sarah Jane, 14. The children both have artistic ability, and the family share a common interest in making music.

*The designer's
first thoughts—
preliminary sketches*

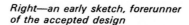

*Right—an early sketch, forerunner
of the accepted design*

The Royal Silver Wedding
An Exercise in Stamp Design

The decision to issue stamps commemorating the Royal Silver Wedding in 1972 was taken by the Post Office in late 1970, when the 'stamp programme' for that year was being drawn up.

First Thoughts and Visuals
Two designers, Broome Lynne and Jeffery Matthews, were commissioned in the first instance to produce ideas based on possible design solutions discussed at their initial briefing with Stuart Rose, Design Adviser at the Post Office and 'director of operations' of the project.

From these, several stamp-sized visuals were prepared and submitted. They included various treatments of the Royal portraits, Royal Family groups, formal calligraphic and inscriptional designs, interior and exterior views of Westminster Abbey and photographs of the wedding.

Eventually four of the designs submitted by Jeffery Matthews were chosen as generally having the right approach and potential for further development, and among these four was a particular favourite of designer Jeffery Matthews, one which was, in fact, practically identical to the finally issued stamp.

The designer had aimed at achieving a design which expressed the highly personal nature of the marriage, but retained a sense of royal dignity and classical simplicity. He considered various ways of reproducing effigies, such as drawings or sculpture, but decided that of all the methods of representation, that of photography seemed the most appropriate.

*Abbey and calligraphic
backgrounds*

*Below—the designer's favourite
visual*

NOVEMBER 1972

SW3

Colour essays—the
accepted profiles in
horizontal format

Interesting alternatives—
¾-face portraits with
backgrounds featuring the
detail of Westminster
Abbey's architecture, in
horizontal and vertical
formats

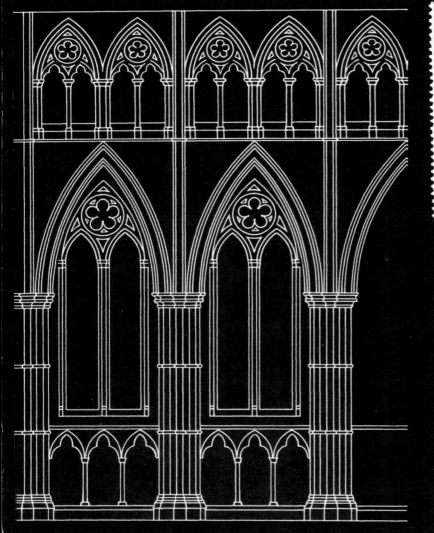

Facing page—further development of the ¾-face
portraits in horizontal format, incorporating the
artist's elegant silver lettering, and the final stages
of the accepted designs in vertical format with
alternative colours and positioning of the inscriptions

Note Duke to be 'darker' tone than Queen

LVER WEDDING

One of Jeffery Matthews' final 'roughs' (above)
for the accepted design, and (below) examples
of his hand-drawn lettering

1947-1972
SILVER WEDDING
2503ᴾ4
Silver Wedding 1947-72

Cameras at the Palace

Norman Parkinson, the photographer, was shown the preliminary designs and briefed on the technical requirements and considerations of the designer and printer, and on the appointed day for the session at Buckingham Palace, he was accompanied by Jeffery Matthews and a representative of Harrison & Sons Ltd. Colour shots were taken ranging from profile to full-face to allow for variations which the designer might wish to make in the minuscule designs. The Queen and the Duke of Edinburgh were photographed separately, and an interesting aspect of the 'Parkinson' technique was the use of a Polaroid 'instant' camera for taking preliminary shots as a check on lighting conditions and suitability of the pose, which could be verified by JM on the spot.

When prints of the new portraits were ready, the designer selected the most suitable ones, and prepared layouts showing precisely how they should be superimposed and positioned within the format of the stamps. Incidentally, this is the first time that a portrait of HRH the Duke of Edinburgh has appeared on a British stamp.

At this stage in the preliminary development of the designs, a number of variations were being considered in both vertical and horizontal formats which included profile portraits, ¾-face portraits, and additional symbolic motifs, such as the architectural details of Westminster Abbey.

Jeffery Matthews prepared hand-drawn lettering for the titling and denomination because he considered that only by so doing could he perfectly integrate the inscription as part of the whole design. His lettering throughout the Silver Wedding project is, indeed, consistently stylish and in sympathy with the event, and his designs for the postmarks, first day cover and pack blend harmoniously with the issued stamps.

Essays in Colour

With photos, layouts and the necessary artwork finally prepared, all was ready for the printers, Harrison & Sons Ltd, to commence 'origination' and produce essays in a variety of colour ways in each of the several designs. These first proofs were shown to the Stamp Advisory Committee (with Matthews present), and the selection narrowed down. With frequent consultation between the designer, George York of Harrisons and Stuart Rose of the Post Office, further proofs were prepared and again submitted to the SAC. This process was repeated on a number of occasions, until the selection was finally reduced to three designs: (1) Profile portraits in vertical format; (2) Profile portraits and (3) ¾-face portraits in horizontal format. The range of colours was narrowed to those which were operationally and aesthetically acceptable, and the printers produced further essays of the three selected designs.

Finally, the essays of these short-listed designs were mounted on dummy first day covers and presentation packs designed by Matthews and on ordinary addressed envelopes, the stamps being mounted singly and in sets of two to give them their proper setting or background. The Stamp Advisory Committee gave its unanimous approval to the designs being recommended to the Palace, where they were subsequently approved by Her Majesty the Queen.

The whole exercise was sustained for over a year and involved the collaboration of a great many talented people.
Compiled from notes contributed by Jeffery Matthews and published with the full co-operation of the Post Office, who also provided the colour photographs of the progressive design essays. The Supplement cover is a photo-enlargement of Mr Matthews' design for the offical first day cover.

The Photographer: Norman Parkinson

Meeting Norman Parkinson was one of those rare experiences one recalls almost in disbelief that it ever really happened. Yet my notes prove that in the short space of 40 minutes on a sultry-hot August afternoon in London, this extremely tall, elegant photographer-extraordinary told me the fascinating story of a career as colourful as the hummingbirds around his home in Tobago or the fashions he photographs for the internationally famous magazine, *Vogue.*

He is 59 and was born in Roehampton, south-west London. On leaving Westminster School, he started in photography when his father apprenticed him to Speaight, the Bond Street photographer, to learn all about portraiture. Becoming impatient with the inadequate pay and with the rôle of studio 'dogsbody', he turned to commercial work, which took him out and about and broadened his experience generally. In 1934, he opened his own studio at No 1 Dover Street, Piccadilly, and in 1945–6 started taking fashion pictures, utilising his increasing skill in portraiture.

In 1949 he was given an exclusive contract by the *Vogue* organisation, a happy arrangement for all concerned and one which will surely continue for many years to come. Fashions in clothes are like stamps—there are always 'new issues' and new designs coming along !

Norman Parkinson has always sought the sun and fresh air, and with his wife and son, now 26, he used to winter in the West Indies—usually in Tobago, the beautiful Caribbean island which lies north-east of Trinidad. Eventually he bought 'a bit of land' there, and built a house. In 1963, he sold his Twickenham house and his farm at Henley-on-Thames, and moved with his family to Tobago, where they arrived in the teeth of a fierce hurricane ! From there he 'commutes' to London and all over the world on his photo assignments for *Vogue.* There are, however, notable exceptions to his world-travel 'routine'.

He was invited to take photographs of Prince Charles in his robes prior to his picturesque Investiture as Prince of Wales in 1969. He also photographed Princess Anne for her 19th birthday in August of that year and, for her 21st birthday—15 August 1971—he took the now famous photographs of Princess Anne which appeared all over the world and in a colour supplement in the London *Evening Standard.*

Harrison & Sons Ltd prepared the all-important colour 'separations' from Norman Parkinson's transparencies for this supplement, and the quality of reproduction was the best he had ever seen in newsprint. It was the success of this commission which made him the natural choice of both Harrisons and the Post Office for the special task of photographing the Queen and the Duke of Edinburgh for the Silver Wedding stamps.

Norman Parkinson's success in photography is not, however, entirely due to expertise and the knack of handling a Hasselblad camera. Equally important is his sympathetic approach to the sitter : for many people, a prolonged sitting before the relentless stare of the camera lens is an ordeal and an embarrassment. To counteract this, he maintains a lively, joking commentary to put the 'victim' at ease and induce a natural, relaxed attitude. I asked him if I should call him a 'fashion' or a 'society' photographer, both being titles attributed to him in the Press, 'Neither', he said. 'I am just a plain photographer'.

He has just one regret—he collected stamps in his younger days and inherited quite a valuable collection from his grandfather. There came the time when he 'needed the cash' and he sold the collection for £120—now he wonders what it would have been worth today . . . Perhaps, however, he will derive some consolation from the fact that the new Silver Wedding stamps will be a permanent reminder to the world at large of his photographic genius.

James Watson

Photo. Barry Weller, Camera Press, London

FDC and Presentation Pack

Jeffery Matthews' design for the first day cover was another exercise in elaborate but controlled calligraphy, and he used the same design for the cover of the presentation pack. Reproduced within the pack are some of the stamps which have had a close personal association with the Royal Family— the Queen's first stamp portrait: the Dorothy Wilding definitive of 1952; Dulac's memorable Coronation portrait of the Queen (1s. 3d., 1953); and Westminster Abbey (2s. 6d., 1966); Windsor Castle (£1, 1955); and Prince Charles' 'Investiture' portrait (1s., 1969).

The Commemorative Postmarks

There was no British stamp for the Royal Wedding in 1947, so that the popular 'Lovers' Knot' postmark used to mark the occasion was an appropriate alternative which captured the hearts of the people. It was used throughout the UK from 20 to 30 November 1947. The design, by a member of the Post Office staff, was also a source of inspiration to Jeffery Matthews, who produced the two delightful postmarks reproduced here. His designs continued the calligraphic theme and, based on true 'love knots', formed a link with the distinctive postmark used 25 years ago.

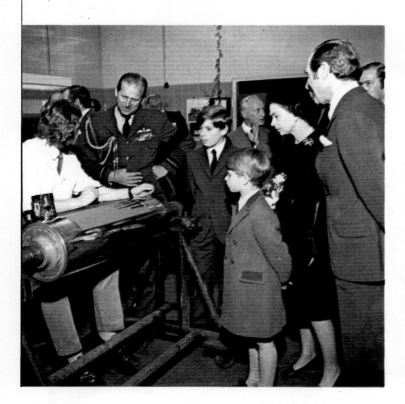

Royal Visit to Harrison & Sons

It had been nearly 20 years since the Queen first visited Harrison's factory at High Wycombe to see the first stamps of her reign being printed. On 30 May 1972, Harrison & Sons Ltd were again honoured by a visit of the Queen and the Duke of Edinburgh, accompanied by their two younger sons, Prince Andrew and Prince Edward. The Royal Family took a particular interest in seeing the 3p Silver Wedding stamps being photogravure-printed on Harrison's new 'Gemini' stamp-printing press. Colour photograph reproduced from *Informe* house magazine of the Harrison Eden Fisher Group.

14 November 1973   3½p

Stamp Portraits of Princess Anne

Not so long ago, a certain well-known postal administration claimed that one of its new issues for the Silver Wedding of the Queen and the Duke of Edinburgh showed Princess Anne on stamps 'for the first time'. They would have been nearer the truth if they had said that their stamps showed the best portrait of the Princess issued up to that time (which indeed it was) for, as many collectors knew, she had appeared on three or four Commonwealth stamps prior to the time of the Silver Wedding.

Princess Anne was born on 15 August 1950, the second child and only daughter of the Queen and the Duke of Edinburgh, at their home at Clarence House, now the London residence of the Queen Mother. Her first stamp portrait appeared in 1952 on one of two Health stamps ($1\frac{1}{2}$d+$\frac{1}{2}$d) issued by New Zealand as part of a regular annual series. The other (2d.+1d.) stamp showed her brother, Prince Charles, HRH the Prince of Wales, at the age of about $3\frac{1}{2}$ years.

Royal Wedding Stamps

A DIARY OF EVENTS

29 May
The Court Circular, issued from Buckingham Palace on Tuesday, 29 May 1973, said
'It is with the greatest pleasure that The Queen and The Duke of Edinburgh announce the betrothal of their beloved daughter The Princess Anne to Lieutenant Mark Phillips, The Queen's Dragoon Guards, son of Mr and Mrs Peter Phillips.'
This announcement set in motion one of the speediest stamp design and production exercises in the history of the British Post Office.

16 June
The Queen gave her formal approval to the issue of a set of two stamps to celebrate the marriage of The Princess Anne to Captain Mark Phillips.

16/18 June
Several designers were briefed to submit preliminary designs on the following themes: heraldic or emblematic designs based on a monogram, miniature painted portraits, photographic portraits, an open-ended graphics brief.

25 June
The preliminary designs of the four designers were shown informally to The Queen and The Princess, with a Post Office recommendation in favour of the photographic treatment by Collis Clements and Edward Hughes.

28 June
The Queen approved the Post Office recommendation, expressing a particular liking for two design treatments on the miniature roughs.
The Palace suggested that the Post Office should look at recent photographs taken of The Princess by Lord Lichfield for her 23rd birthday.

29 June
Possible portraits were selected by the designers and Lord Lichfield was commissioned to take photographs of Captain Phillips in Germany at the first opportunity after his return from Australia on 22 July. It was then thought unlikely that there would be an opportunity to photograph The Princess and Captain Phillips together within the available production time.

4 July
The Stamp Advisory Committee approved the progress so far made.

19 July
A briefing meeting for the photographic session in Germany on the following Sunday was held between Lord Lichfield; Collis Clements, one of the designers; George York, Production Director of Harrison's; and Stuart Rose, Post Office Design Adviser.

20 July
It was learned from the Palace that The Princess and Captain Phillips would both be at Windsor on the evening of Sunday 22 July. Permission was graciously given for Lord Lichfield to photograph them together on that evening.

22 July
Photographs taken at Windsor Castle.

23 July
Contact prints shown to the Post Office and the designers, and a selection made for essaying.

27 July
Final artwork approved by the Post Office and sent to Harrison's the printers.

2 August
First proofs seen at Harrison's by the Post Office and the designers. From nineteen colourways proofed, two pairs were chosen for submission to the Palace, with a recommendation for certain improvements in detail to be made before printing.

3 August
Proofs submitted to the Palace.

6 August
The Queen approves the Post Office's recommended set with the proposed modifications.

8 August
The stamps go to press.

Those portraits were taken from photographs by Marcus Adams, the court photographer, and that of Princess Anne is of especial interest because it bears a striking resemblance to the first stamp portrait of the Queen herself, which appeared on a charming Newfoundland 6 c. stamp of 1932. This portrait also was adapted from photographs by Marcus Adams, showing the young Princess Elizabeth (as she then was) at the age of 4, holding a toy parrot, her hair a mass of blonde curls.

Since 1954, when Princess Anne was taken with Prince Charles to meet their parents on their return from a Commonwealth tour at Tobruk, Libya, and visited Malta and Gibraltar, she has travelled abroad on numerous occasions, usually accompanying the Queen and the Duke of Edinburgh on their official—and sometimes unofficial—visits overseas. Commonwealth countries seldom miss an opportunity of issuing 'Royal Visit' stamps and these have provided the few existing portraits of Princess Anne.

In 1970 she accompanied the Queen and the Duke on their spring tour of Fiji, Tonga, New Zealand and Australia. From Fiji they sailed for Tonga in the Royal Yacht *Britannia* (on which Princess Anne and Captain Mark Phillips will spend their honeymoon in the Caribbean), and for this fleeting visit Tonga issued a dozen or so stamps of the self-adhesive type, designed by M. Meers and depicting members of the British and Tongan Royal Families, each group portrayed in gold 'picture frames'. The left-hand group comprised the Queen, the Duke and Princess Anne, while

that on the right showed King Taufu'ahau Tupou IV, his wife and daughter.

In New Zealand the Royal entourage was joined by the Prince of Wales, and the visit was commemorated, not by New Zealand herself, but by the Cook Islands with the issue of three stamps (on 12 June), one of which, the 5 c., showed a composite picture of the Queen, the Duke, Princess Anne and the Prince of Wales from a design by Victor Whiteley, inscribed 'ROYAL VISIT MARCH 1970'. During February and March 1971, the Duke of Edinburgh again toured the Pacific *en route* to Australia, and the Cook Islands marked the occasion with a set of five stamps and a miniature sheet. Among the designs, which were based on photographs, principally of Prince Philip, was the 4 c. which depicted the Royal Family, including Princess Anne, on the terrace at Windsor Castle, a happy family picture.

So we come to last year's Silver Wedding and it was again the Cook Islands (and Aitutaki) which recaptured some of the nostalgia and romance of the original wedding of the Queen (as Princess Elizabeth) and Lieutenant Philip Mountbatten, RN, which took place at Westminster Abbey in November (the wedding month!) 1947. The most impressive of the Cook stamps was the 30 c. which showed the official wedding group at Buckingham Palace, the bride and groom flanked by King George VI and Queen Elizabeth, Queen Mary, Princess Alice of Battenberg (Philip's mother), Princess Alice and, among the bridesmaids, Princesses Margaret and Alexandra.

Britain, Guernsey, Jersey and 30 Commonwealth territories (besides the Cook Islands) issued stamps for the Royal Silver Wedding. With commendable enthusiasm, Jersey commemorated the event with four attractive stamps featuring the Royal Family, designed by Gordon Drummond from photographs by Desmond Groves, one of the world's leading photographers whose pictures of the Queen and the Duke were also selected for the Commonwealth designs. The Jersey 2½p pictured a smiling Princess Anne, who also appeared in the family group on the 20p stamp.

It is perhaps appropriate to recall that some splendid photographs of Princess Anne were taken by another celebrated photographer, Norman Parkinson, on the occasion of her 21st birthday—colour photographs which were published all over the world and in the form of a special colour supplement in the London *Evening Standard*. It was as a result of this commission that 'Parks' (as he is known) was selected to photograph the Queen and the Duke for the GB Silver Wedding stamps.

Now we come bang up-to-date with the Royal Wedding of HRH Princess Anne and Captain Mark Phillips, due to take place at Westminster Abbey on the 14th of this month. Stamp designers and printers have been working at top pressure to produce the wedding stamps for Britain, Guernsey, Jersey, the Isle of Man and 22 or more Commonwealth territories.

All, except the striking GB full-face pictures, designed by Collis Clements and Ted Hughes of Maidstone, Kent, from specially-commissioned photographs, appear to have a common source—photographs taken on the day in May 1973 following the announcement of the engagement, when the Princess and her fiancé appeared on the lawns of Buckingham Palace for the official photographers.

What the stamp pictures do not show, however, is the Princess's engagement ring—every young girl's dream—a sapphire flanked by diamonds, glittering on her finger!

James Watson

The six heads made from Photograph No. O 15957 D.

STAMP PORTRAITS
OF
THE QUEEN

By CYRIL R. H. PARSONS

NOW that three years have elapsed since the accession of Her Majesty, and that the Dominions and a representative group of the Crown Colonies have replaced stamps showing a portrait of King George VI by one of the reigning Sovereign, it is desirable to record details of the sources of the stamp portraits. In this article an attempt has been made to trace the origins of the portraits which have appeared up to the time of writing, and to discuss briefly the differences between the various engravings reproduced from the same originals.

There are four firms of stamp printers in England, and these, together with the various government printers in the Dominions, using three different processes (typography, photogravure and recess-printing) have each reproduced photographs of the Queen on their various stamps. Almost all the photographs so used were by Dorothy Wilding, Ltd. of London, and their descriptions form the greater part of this article, the exceptions being listed at the end.

The resulting stamp portraits often differ from each other by virtue of the different printers, who use their own

techniques in transferring the original photograph to their particular media. In some instances the general outline and arrangement of the original has been altered or " developed ".

The following procedure is probably adopted by the printers of the recess-printed stamps, in order to reproduce the same portrait on different stamps. An engraver's drawing is prepared from the photograph, indicating the lines to be engraved to give the required effect. With this as a guide, a " key portrait die " is engraved and then transferred to the master die for the particular stamp. The steel printing plates are finally produced from the master die. The existence of the " engraver's

drawing " is indicated by the fact that Waterlow produced more than one size of head, with very similar shading lines, from all the principal photographs. These similar engravings, of different sizes could, alternatively, be obtained by means of the pantograph technique. The subject and general lay-out of the main design of the stamp would probably account for the differences in background, and variation in minor details, from one stamp to another.

For convenience, the stamps concerned may be divided into three arbitrary groups, according to the type of portrait :

(a) those in which the Queen wears a diadem,
(b) those in which she wears a tiara, and
(c) those in which she is bareheaded.

Some notes on the first two groups may be appropriate.

The portrait on the current stamps of Great Britain shows the Queen wearing what is officially described as " A diadem' or regal circlet of diamonds. Four cross pattées and four rose, shamrock and thistle motifs. Two rows of pearls in lower band." The diadem was designed by and made for King George IV

The three heads made from Photograph No. O 15957 E.

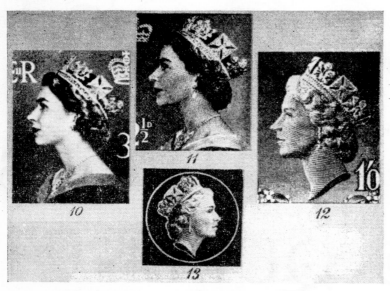

The four heads made from **Photograph No. O 15957 F.**

who intended it to be worn over a Cap of State (the velvet cap worn inside a crown). This is not the first appearance of this diadem in the stamp album, as Queen Victoria wore it when Chalon painted his famous portrait, the head of which was reproduced on many mid-Victorian stamps. The present Queen first wore it in public for the opening of Parliament in November 1952. She also wore it on the way to her Coronation and at the beginning of the service.

The Crown Colonies' Coronation stamps show the Queen wearing " A diamond scroll tiara with diamond points." This tiara was given to Queen Mary by " the young ladies of Great Britain and Ireland " on the occasion of her marriage in 1893. She, in turn, gave it to the Queen for her wedding in 1947.

In the following discussion of the various portraits, reference is made to twelve different photographs. Tables are provided showing the different engravings, together with the catalogue numbers of stamps so far issued, on which they have been reproduced. For convenience in comparing different engravings, Figures 1 to 39 have all been given the same enlargement, namely twice the linear size of the stamps. In photogravure stamps, differences in the size of the portrait involve only a variation in photographic enlargement of the same original and for this reason have not been considered as new versions.

PORTRAITS WITH DIADEM

Six photographs by Dorothy Wilding, showing the Queen wearing the diadem, have been reproduced on stamps. Their reference numbers are O 15957 D, E, F, H, Z and Y.

Photograph No. O 15957 D.
This is a three-quarter face portrait looking left, and was used only by the four British printing firms. There are five engraved versions and one in photogravure, as indicated in the following table :

Bradbury, Wilkinson

Fig. 1. Cayman Islands, S.G. 149, 150, 151, 154, 156, 157, 159, 160. Fiji, S.G. 296, 297. Montserrat, S.G. 144, 145, 148. Southern Rhodesia,[1] S.G. 78, 79, 84, 87, 89, 90.
Fig. 2. New Zealand, S.G. 723 to 730.

De La Rue

Fig. 3. Fiji, S.G. 279, 288. Gibraltar, S.G. 146, 147, 150, 151, 152, 153, 155, 159.

Waterlow

Fig. 4. Malta, S.G. 262. St. Kitts-Nevis, S.G. 107 to 118.
Fig. 5. Fiji, S.G. 289, 295.

Harrison

Fig. 6. Mauritius, S.G. 297, 297a, 298, 300, 301, 302. North Borneo, S.G. 380. Seychelles, S.G. 174, 177, 178, 179, 181, 182, 184, 187, 188.

The engraving on Bradbury, Wilkinson's first head is by means of bold dotted lines not very close together : there is much diagonal cross-hatching on the Queen's right cheek and also by her left ear. The lines on the cheek and neck run diagonally downwards, away from the nose. On their second por-

trait, the dotted lines and the cross-hatching on the right cheek are finer ; and the shading on the left cheek and neck is by means of more and closer lines running from N.W. to S.E. The cross-hatching by the left ear is absent.

De La Rue's head contains many more lines, mostly dotted. On the neck the shading first runs slightly up from the left, and then flattens out. The cross-hatching on the right cheek is by fine, continuous lines close together.

Waterlow's two versions, which only differ in size, have bold lines widely separated. The shading on the Queen's left cheek runs approximately N.W. to S.E., but the shading on the neck is from N.E. to S.W. The cross-hatching on her left cheek is not so pronounced as in the other versions.

Photograph No. O 15957 E.
There is not much difference between the head of the first photograph and that of the next, No. O 15957 E, which has been reproduced on the Coronation and definitive series for Great Britain and the locally-printed Coronation stamps of Australia and South Africa[2] ; the most obvious is that the shoulders are at a different angle. The notable feature of the Australian head is that much shading is by means of continuous lines with dots interspersed. The detail of Harrison's photogravure head on the British stamps is far sharper than that on the South African Coronation stamp, although the latter is twice the size. In fact, the British stamps give one of the clearest reproductions of the diadem for the whole group.

O 15957 H

Photograph No. O 15957 H.
By courtesy of Dorothy Wilding, Ltd.

The portraits made from photographs Nos. O 15957 H and Z.

The three versions are as follows :

Harrison

Fig. 7. Great Britain, S.G. 515 to 531, **532,** 533, 535.

Australian Govt. Printer

Fig. 8. Australia, S.G. 264 to 266.

S. African Govt. Printer

Fig. 9. South Africa, S.G. 143, 143a.

Photograph No. O 15957 F. This is a side face portrait looking left and has been used for the Australian definitive set and also for the New Zealand Coronation 3d. and similar designs for the Dependencies, produced by Harrison in photogravure. Although the engraving of the shoulder-length portrait on the lower values of the Australian set is different from that of the sculptured head of the 1/o½d., it is obvious that they were both developed from the same original. It would also seem that the small head on the American Memorial stamp is a reversed version of the same portrait. In this portrait, it can be seen that the diadem is indeed a complete " circlet ".

The four versions of this portrait are as follows :

Harrison

Fig. 10. New Zealand, S.G. 715. Cook Is., S.G. 160. Niue, S.G. 123. Samoa, S.G. 229. Tokelau, S.G. 4.

Australian Govt. Printer

Fig. 11. Australia, S.G. 261 to 263a.
Fig. 12. Australia, S.G. 282.
Fig. 13. Australia, S.G. 283.

Photograph No. O 15957 H. This is a shoulder-length three-quarter face portrait, looking right and reproduced, so far, only on the New Zealand middle values of the current set. Many collectors will probably regard this engraving as the best of all those made for stamps, both from the point of view of the quality of the work and of its likeness to the Queen.

De La Rue

Fig. 14. New Zealand, S.G. 731 to 733.

Photograph No. O 15957 Z. A three-quarter length portrait looking right, rather similar to portrait H, but turned a little more to the right and differing in the position of the Queen's arms. The Australian Govt. Printer made the only version of this portrait.[2]

Australian Govt. Printer

Fig. 15. Australia, S.G. 273.

Photograph No. O 15957 Y. The Ceylon Coronation issue is the only stamp showing a full face portrait of the Queen, wearing the diadem, and was developed by Bradbury, Wilkinson from photograph No. O 15957 Y. Here the detail of the " rose, shamrock and thistle motif ", in the diadem, has been rather neglected.

Bradbury, Wilkinson

Fig. 16. Ceylon, S.G. 433.

Photograph No. O 15957 Z.
By courtesy of Dorothy Wilding, Ltd.

PORTRAITS WITH TIARA

Photograph No. O 15924 I. Most of the stamp portraits, showing the Queen wearing the tiara, are taken from photograph No. O 15924 I, which is a three-quarter face photograph looking right.[3] There are seven recess-printed versions and two versions in photogravure, as enumerated in the table below :

The only head made from photograph No. O 15957 Y.

Bradbury, Wilkinson

Fig. 17. Crown Colonies Coronation. Bahamas, S.G. 201 to 216. Cayman Islands, S.G. 148, 152, 153, 155, 158, 161. Grenada, S.G. 192 to 201. Montserrat, S.G. 137, 138, 139, 140, 141, 142, 143, 146, 147, 149. Sarawak, S.G. 188. Somaliland, S.G. 137 to 147. Southern Rhodesia, S.G. 80, 81, 82, 83, 85, 86, 88, 91.

De La Rue

Fig. 18. Kenya, S.G. 169.
Fig. 19. Fiji, S.G. 283, 287. Gambia, S.G. 171 to 185. Gibraltar, S.G. 145, 148, 149, 154, 156, 157, 158.

Waterlow

Fig. 20. Bechuanaland, S.G. 143 to 153. Falkland Is., S.G. 139. Fiji, S.G. 280, 292, 292a, 294. Jamaica, S.G. 154.
Fig. 21. Rhodesia & Nyasaland,[2] S.G. 1 to 9.
Fig. 22. Rhodesia & Nyasaland,[2] S.G. 10 to 15.

Canadian Bank Note Co.

Fig. 23. Canada.

Harrison

Fig. 24. Dominica, S.G. 140. Mauritius, S.G. 293, 294, 295, 296, 299, 302a, 303, 303a, 304, 305, 306. North Borneo, S.G. 372, 375, 376, 377, 378, 379, 381, 383. Seychelles, S.G. 175, 176, 180, 183, 185, 186.

S. African Govt. Printer

Fig. 25. South West Africa,[3] S.G. 149 to 153.

In Bradbury, Wilkinson's head, all the dotted lines of shading run downwards to either side of the nose. The lines on the Queen's neck run upwards from left to right. De La Rue's shoulder-length portrait on the Kenya £1 (169) is similar : there are, however, more dotted shading lines which are lighter. On the other hand, their second version has been engraved with cheek lines curved upwards to the nose and ear, with the lowest point in the centre of the cheek. The lines on the neck run

The nine heads made from photographs Nos. O 15924 I and CC.

was produced at very short notice "from a portrait approved by Her Majesty for use on some other stamps designed by the Crown Agents." As far as the writer can ascertain, no Crown Colonies' stamps include this portrait, so reference was probably being made to the New Zealand stamps.

The two versions of this portrait are the following :

De La Rue
Fig. 26. New Zealand, S.G. 714, 716.
Fig. 27. S. Rhodesia, S.G. 77.

PORTRAITS WITH BARE HEAD

Photograph No. O 15924 A. To date, the portraits with bare head have all been profiles facing right or left. Those looking left, were developed from photograph No. O 15924 A. Details of the use of the seven different engravings are given below :

Bradbury, Wilkinson
Fig. 28. Barbados, S.G. 290, 292, 293, 294, 295. Bermuda, S.G. 135 to 150. Dominica, S.G. 144, 145, 146, 147, 148, 149, 153, 154. Gold Coast, S.G. 153, 153a, 159, 160, 161, 162, 163. Nyasaland, S.G. 173, 173a, 175, 178, 180, 181, 184, 185, 187. Trinidad & Tobago, S.G. 269, 270, 271, 272, 273, 275, 276, 277, 277a, 278.

De La Rue
Fig. 29. Basutoland, S.G. 43 to 53. Ceylon, S.G. 434. Jamaica, S.G. 156, 158. Kenya, S.G. 160 to 168. St. Helena, S.G. 153 to 165. Tristan da Cunha, S.G. 14 to 27.

De La Rue (typo.)
Fig. 30. Leeward Islands, S.G. 117 to 129.

The two heads made from photograph No. O 15924 O.

downwards from left to right. These three versions are all reasonably light.

Waterlow's versions also resemble, to some extent, that made by Bradbury, Wilkinson, except that the dotted lines are much heavier and there are horizontal lines on the chin. The shading on the neck is by means of diagonal cross-hatching. Their head on the Crown Colonies' stamps differs from that on those from Rhodesia and Nyasaland in that on the former the continuous lines on the Queen's right cheek curve slightly in, towards the ear, while on the latter they are almost straight. Also, the Rhodesian stamps show the hair parting to be more nearly horizontal. The head on the higher values of the Rhodesian series (S.G. 10–15) is very similar to that on the lower values, except that it is larger.

The Canadian Bank Note Company's

version has some continuous lines running from the middle of the cheek downwards towards the ear, and also below the chin. There is diagonal shading, with fine lines and thicker dotted lines on the neck. Little comment can be passed on the photogravure versions as they are exact photographic reproductions of the original.

Photograph No. O 15924 O. De La Rue produced the head on the New Zealand Coronation 2d. and 4d. stamps from photograph No. O 15924 O, a three-quarter face portrait looking left, and the engraving on this head, although much smaller, follows the same general lines as that on the Southern Rhodesian Coronation stamp,[2] which was also printed by De La Rue. All that the Rhodesia and Nyasaland authorities would state about the latter was that it

The seven heads made from photograph No. O 15924 A.

The head by Bradbury, Wilkinson has the cheek shading by means of light dotted lines widely separated and running slightly downwards from left to right. The lines on the neck are almost horizontal. The recess-printed head by De La Rue has close and heavy dotted lines on the face and neck which run from N.W. to S.E. Their typographed head, in two sizes, has continuous heavy lines running approximately horizontally across the face and neck. The versions by Waterlow, in three sizes, have widely-spaced heavy dotted lines going approximately from N.W. to S.E. on the face. The shading on the neck runs upwards from left to right. There is more extensive cross-hatching on the neck than on the recess-printed versions by the two other printers.

Photograph No. O 15924 Z. All the profiles, facing right, are based on photograph No. O 15924 Z.[4] The allocation of the five versions is as follows :

The dotted lines on the head by Bradbury, Wilkinson first run slightly downwards from the nose to the centre of the cheek, where they turn suddenly, almost vertically, towards the neck, where they follow the same general direction. De La Rue's version has more, finer lines close together. They run from N.E. to S.W. across the face. The shading on the neck follows the other diagonal. Waterlow's head, again in three sizes, has interrupted lines going in a direction of about N.E. to S.W., across the face. There is, however, some diagonal cross-hatching on the neck, which is absent from the other two versions.

This completes the list of stamps issued to date reproducing portraits by Dorothy Wilding Ltd. If any have escaped our careful check, apologies are

[The five heads made from photographs Nos. O 15924 Z and N.]

tendered in advance with the request that they be kindly brought to the Editor's attention.

The few remaining portraits of the Queen which have appeared on stamps were from photographs from various sources as follows :

Canada, S.G. 450 to 460. From a photograph by Karsh, of Ottawa.

Canada, S.G. 461. From a bas-relief model by Emanuel Hahn, probably based on photograph No. O 15924 A.

New Zealand, S.G. 721. From a portrait on the cover of *Our Young Queen*, published by Pitkins.

New Zealand, S.G. 734 to 736. From a press photograph.

The writer wishes to acknowledge the assistance, so willingly given by the following, in supplying the data which made the article possible : the General Post Offices in London and the Dominions, the Dominions' High Commissioners in London, the Crown Agents, Bradbury, Wilkinson and Dorothy Wilding Ltd. ; also the authorities at Buckingham Palace for details of the diadem and tiara. It is regretted, however, that the original portraits, with the exception of the two shown, could not be reproduced in this article as they have not yet been released for publication.

---

[1]The printers stated that the head on these Southern Rhodesian stamps was based on photograph No. O 15957 E, but the angle of the shoulders and the similarity of the engraving indicate that it was developed from No. O 15957 D, as shown.

[2]The number of the photograph from which this version was developed was unknown to the authorities, but is given here as a result of consultation with Dorothy Wilding, Ltd.

[3]There is a second photograph, No. O 15924 CC, which is very similar, except in that it has a darker background. Only the South West Africa Director of Posts and Telegraphs reported a number which bore any similarity to it (O 15924 CE), for the South West African Coronation, and it is doubtful if the photograph was reproduced on any other stamps, even though some of the engraved portraits have noticeably darker backgrounds.

[4]There is a second photograph, No. O 15924 N, which is almost identical. The New Zealand Official stamps were reported to be developed from it, but the engraved head is identical with the profile on Bradbury, Wilkinson's Crown Colonies' stamps developed from photograph No. O 15924 Z.

GIBBONS STAMP MONTHLY

EDITED BY STANLEY PHILLIPS
AND C. P. RANG VOL. XXVI JULY 1, 1953 No. 11 PUBLISHED PRICE
SIXPENCE NET

The Coronation Stamps

GREAT BRITAIN

THE four stamps commemorating the Queen's Coronation, appearing on the morning after the ceremonies whose splendours were still in our minds, made for stamp collectors another happy day. They were first placed on sale at one minute after midnight on the morning of June 3rd at the two all-night London post offices of Leicester Square and St. Martin's le Grand. According to the Postmaster-General the earliest collection thereafter would be at about 3 a.m. which would be the hour shown on the earliest possible postmarks. The stamps are to remain on sale until the end of October. No booklets of them are to be made.

About seventy designs were submitted by selected artists who had been invited to compete. An advisory panel chose the best and the final approval was given by the Queen.

The 2½d. seems to command preference and in this the popular choice is justified by the better composition ; the larger head occupies the correct area of the stamp and the retention of the light background of the portrait as in the original photograph avoids the false reflections seen in the 4d. The arrangement of the Regalia, though giving it prominence, rightly leaves the portrait as the main feature. The stamp was designed by Mr. Edgar G. Fuller, born 1898, trained at the Brighton School of Art and since 1923 a heraldic artist for the College of Arms, London. He is the designer of the reverse of the new five-shilling coin.

The 4d. is interesting as an example of the same idea as the 2½d. but much less happily treated. It gives the impression of a collection of bits and pieces, separately drawn and then fitted together. The cut-out appearance of the head is not good and the placing of a crown above a diadem appears anomalous. The designer was Mr. Michael Goaman, 31, a free-lance designer who studied at Reading University Art School and the Central School of Arts and Crafts.

The 1s. 3d. stands out from the others on account of its different portrait. It was in fact not intended to be a portrait, but in the Postmaster-General's words, a purely symbolic design of the crowned

Queen against a Tudor tapestry background. It was designed by Mr. Edmund Dulac, who was also responsible for the last Coronation stamp, and completed only shortly before he died last May.

The fourth stamp of the set, the 1s. 6d. was designed by Mr. M. C. Farrar-Bell who also designed the current 2½d. of the permanent series. It is the only stamp of the set to include the date of the Coronation but is not otherwise noteworthy.

To round off the philatelic commemoration of the Coronation the Post Office also used from the same

hour as the stamps the special postmark shown here. It was designed by the Engineering Department of the Post Office.

CROWN COLONIES

Collectors will have every reason to be pleased with the set for the colonies. The simple and dignified design of which we had only a sample some time ago is most attractive when repeated on some 62 stamps. The gentle variations of the frame shades are nicely brought out by the centre, black throughout ; in fact, an attractive arrangement of these stamps is to ignore the alphabetical order and to group them by their colours, green, purple, blue, grey, orange, red, brown and violet, when all the variations of shade will be revealed.

AUSTRALIA

Quite a pleasing and well engraved portrait of the Queen, but the superimposition of the lettering on the crown leaves both rather muddled.

CANADA

A cold violet is not the best colour to convey the warmth of feeling engendered by the Coronation. This and the poor likeness of the Queen cause

one to react unfavourably to this stamp but it must be said for it that the design is quite attractive.

CEYLON

Not what could be called an inspired composition but the Queen's portrait is one of the most pleasing.

NEW ZEALAND

Though rather a mixture of styles this set will appeal to many as a simple pictorial arrangement of all the popular ingredients of the Coronation. The Queen's portrait on the 3d. is very effective.

SOUTH AFRICA

Quite a pleasing composition.

SOUTHERN RHODESIA

As the largest of all the Coronation stamps and the highest in face value this 2s. 6d. stamp is immediately

striking. It is also a splendid piece of engraving and would perhaps have been the best stamp of the series had the Queen been given a more smiling countenance.

SOUTH WEST AFRICA

Although not strictly connected with the Coronation the flowers with which each stamp is differently ornamented would have given them a special interest, but unfortunately they are so weak as to be hardly recognizable as flowers. The general effect of the issue is otherwise favourable.

C.P.R.

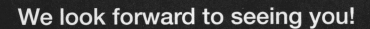